Ross Reyburn is a journalist on the *Birmingham Post*, the co-author of Wallace Reyburn's *World of Rugby* and *Crash Tackle*, and is a keen sportsman. Mike Emery is a former London journalist who now concentrates on his twin obsessions – squash and cycle-racing. Both authors have known Jonah Barrington for many years, playing squash at the West Warwickshire Squash Club where he trains.

Jonah

The official biography of Jonah Barrington

ROSS REYBURN & MICHAEL EMERY

SPHERE BOOKS LIMITED
London and Sydney

First Published in Great Britain by
J. M. Dent & Sons Ltd 1983
Copyright © Ross Reyburn and Michael Emery 1983
Published by Sphere Books Ltd 1985
30–32 Gray's Inn Road, London WC1X 8JL
Cover photograph © Robin Eley Jones 1985

**TRADE
MARK**

Set in 9½ on 10½ Linotron Times

Printed and bound in Great Britain by
Cox & Wyman Ltd, Reading

Contents

Acknowledgments

This book could not have been written without the full co-operation of Jonah Barrington, who made himself available for interviews for six months. We are also very grateful for the help provided by: Madeline Barrington, Nicholas Barrington, Rex Bellamy, Edna Brown, Michael Chamberlayne, Michael Corby, Pilly Cowell, Raymond Francis, Malcolm Hamer, Bomber Harris, Ken Hiscoe, John Horry MBE, Geoff Hunt, Azam Khan, Paul Millman, Bob Morris, Cam Nancarrow, Geraldine Richmond-Watson, Dicky Rutnagur, Dr Craig Sharp, Jack Sweetman, Count Nikolai Tolstoy and David Wild. We would especially like to thank members of the Barrington family, and Count Tolstoy, for the loan of photographs from their private collections.

We would also like to thank photographers Gerry Cranham, Robin Eley Jones and Ken Kelly, and All Sport, The Birmingham Post & Mail, The Daily Mirror Library, Ealing Squash Club, the Morwenstow Society, The Times Library and Ian Wright for the newspaper cuttings, photographs and statistics provided for the book. And the following books also provided invaluable background information: *Barrington on Squash* by Jonah Barrington (Stanley Paul, 1973), *The Book of Jonah* by Jonah Barrington with Clive Everton (Stanley Paul, 1972), *The History of Squash Rackets* by John Horry MBE (A.C.M. Webb, 1979), *Murder on the Squash Court* by Jonah Barrington with Angela Padmore (Stanley Paul, 1982), *The Story of Squash* by Rex Bellamy (Cassell, 1978) and *Tackle Squash* by Jonah Barrington with John Hopkins (Stanley Paul, 1977).

Ross Reyburn and Michael Emery. April, 1983

Jonah

1. The Living Legend

In another age, you would probably have found him leading a cavalry charge, battling across the unexplored Antarctic wastelands or destroying the Luftwaffe in a Battle of Britain Spitfire. But in the 1960s mowing down the Dervish was definitely out of fashion, few challenges remained for the explorer and there were no gentlemanly wars left to fight. So Jonah Barrington set out to become the only thing he could – a sporting hero – and the manner in which he achieved it was quite remarkable.

In the London of the 1960s, many of his contemporaries were staging a revolt against convention, creating what *Time* magazine described in a now-famous phrase as 'Swinging London'. But while others of his generation were more concerned with music, parties, drinking, drugs and overturning traditional attitudes, Barrington decided to ignore the temptations of the world's most exciting city in order to live like a Trappist monk. With a single-mindedness rare among British sportsmen, he simply decided that his future would centre on a lighted cave known as a squash court and that he would become the best squash player in the world – a remarkable ambition for a young man who had showed no outstanding sporting ability during his schooldays at Cheltenham College or later at Trinity College, Dublin.

But in a remarkable twenty-six months, Barrington was to become what one journalist described as 'the fittest man in the world', achieving the first step on the road to his ambition during the winter of 1966-7 by becoming the first Briton to win both the British Open and the British Amateur Championship in the same season. Guided by his Pakistani coach, Nasrullah Khan, the man who at one time was barely able to make the Cornwall county team was to win the British Open, the squash equivalent of Wimbledon, six times in seven years.

For Barrington, the son of a soldier and firm believer in genetic inheritance, squash was just another form of warfare. In his own words: 'It may be more civilised than actual warfare but the two are nonetheless analogous. That is not to say there is no such thing as "social sport" – sport for fun, to make friends – but there is an enormous difference between "social sport" and high-level, professional international sport. There is no life-and-death struggle for those who play sport for fun. Sportsmen are actually militants. We are peacetime soldiers. Had I been a professional soldier like my father, I am sure I would have looked upon war as a theatre of advancement where courage and valour were always rewarded – and I would have wanted to win. Losing is shame, despair and frustration.'

Perhaps even more remarkable than Barrington's achievements on the squash court has been his extraordinary influence on the game. Almost single-handedly he created the British squash boom in the 1970s, becoming the sport's first superstar and raising its level from that of an obscure gentlemanly pastime to that of a sport enjoyed by more than 2,500,000 Britons. Part of Barrington's appeal was his interesting background. The second son of an eccentric retired army officer, he was brought up in the remote parish of Morwenstow in the north-east corner of Cornwall, developing in the process an intense sporting rivalry with his elder brother, Nicholas. After attending prep school in Ireland, he led an intensely miserable existence at the English public school, Cheltenham College, suffering a nervous breakdown when he was only fourteen. Later he was to squander much of his university career in the pubs of Dublin. However, his arrival in London in 1964 produced a dramatic transformation in his lifestyle. The drinker drank no more and, after a long succession of part-time jobs, he decided, with an uncharacteristic single-mindedness, to devote all his time to his training and squash. In 1966, having amazed the sporting world by achieving the coveted British Open, the press found itself unable to resist the incongruity of this early background or his undoubted charisma and readiness to speak his mind. Thus he ensured an unprecedented amount of publicity not only for himself but also for the sport, becoming, in the process, the greatest squash evangelist of his time – and a controversial figure who aroused a considerable level of interest among the general public.

Turning professional in 1969 was a gamble in a field that had previously provided negligible financial rewards. But this all-important decision, based on ambition and resolve, was to make Barrington a wealthy man. Today he lives in an attractive Edwardian country home set in five acres of grounds near Solihull, a few miles from Birmingham, with his wife, Madeline, and their two sons, Nicholas and Jonah. The property is worth in the region of £250,000 and, with a new five-year sponsorship contract recently signed with Dunlop, together with the income from his highly popular squash clinics, he now probably earns more than £60,000 a year despite the fact that he is now over 40 and can no longer count himself among the world's top players.

These rewards, however, are certainly no more than he deserves. In fact they could be termed small in the context of his achievements and the scale of effort involved. In other sports, for instance boxing, few resent the millions earned by top heavyweight fighters like Ali and Frazier, for these were exceptional athletes richly articulate in a dangerous language. Set against such yardsticks, how can the vastly inflated sums paid to even mediocre footballers, golfers, tennis players and cricketers possibly be justified?

After Borg had won Wimbledon for the umpteenth time, the press revealed that he had been offered a million pounds by Dunlop merely to use their tennis rackets in Europe . . . an offer he politely declined after a rival company offered more. Now Borg is an exceptional athlete and tennis player but certainly he would have striven no harder for his fame than did Barrington. Just one example of the imbalance existing in endorsement payments before Barrington's astonishing impact on the world of squash is typified in his early dealings with Dunlop: 'In 1970 I had just won the British Open for the fourth time and Dunlop wrote to me asking if I was interested in endorsing their rackets for another year. Obviously I was, but as I had just won yet another Open, and for the fourth time, I enquired of them if they might consider raising my fee from £1,000 to £2,500. Being careful to congratulate me on my recent achievement, they responded to my request, saying "Come, come, old chap, there has to be a limit you know!"'

Can you imagine what a Wimbledon champion would have been offered even then to endorse the products of a British racket manufacturer? Squash club proprietors throughout the world who now make handsome profits, and the tennis-style troupe of touring professionals who today earn decent rewards from the sport, have good reason to be grateful to Barrington. For it was his vision of a game that would one day be played by millions, followed by his instigation of a tournament squash circuit for the professionals, that has enabled them to enjoy those rewards today. Without Barrington, squash for the pros would have been like golf before Walter Hagen. They would still be teaching housewives, stringing rackets and forbidden entry to the clubhouse.

In order to fight what must sadly be a losing battle with time, Barrington continues to keep himself in top condition for his clinics and exhibition matches, even though most people may consider it beyond even his powers to make a realistic return to the competitive circuit, which has been denied him, on account of injuries, for nearly two years. But his obsessive worship of the cult of fitness continues at an age when injuries seem to come in twos and threes, and constant medical attention is necessary to keep him functioning even at a level where he can practise honourably with some of the world's leading players.

'Heat is what we crave, heat is what we crave,' he repeated at a training session not so long ago. And by heat, he *means* heat. Visit one of the squash clubs in Birmingham he uses as a training camp and if the courts are stiflingly hot, you know that Jonah is not far away. At one club he rapidly discovered how to 'adjust' the 'tamper-proof' thermostat with a judicious poke or two with a long enough pen or pencil. The club, alarmed at their rapidly soaring heating bills, fitted an anti-Jonah device. But the solution was simple: he moved his training to a neighbouring club with a sauna room where he was able to warm-up for his warm-up. To this day, when the session is over, the craving for heat continues and a routine is religiously observed, whatever the weather. His training partner, Bomber Harris, collects the car and brings it to the door where Barrington will only join him once the engine is warm and the heater is operating at full blast.

A cold is a serious illness with Barrington – 'flu positively terminal. He will never venture near anyone who has a cold and, on one of those rare occasions when he himself is stricken, he refuses even to shake hands with anybody for fear of transmitting the dreaded condition.

Cigarettes he regards with dread and disgust. Perhaps this is understandable when you know that both his parents died from cancer. Smoking in his presence is a complete non-starter. One colleague recalls the day he wandered into a changing room to find Barrington sitting there after a heavy training session with the window wide open. The man obsessed with heat had the window open? Why? 'It's your friend,' came the reply. 'He's been smoking. Here. In this room.' And, added Barrington accusingly, 'I know *you're* partial to the odd cigarette, too,' happily unaware he was speaking to a 40-a-day man.

Perhaps you may be getting the impression that Barrington's obsession with fitness approaches paranoiac proportions. Without doubt, you would be right. His attitude is typified by a story told in loud whispers throughout Midland squash circles of the time when Jonah's wife, Madeline, was expecting their second child. The former athlete was in her early forties, a sensitive age for a woman to be having a baby. Obviously Madeline had to be more closely monitored than a younger woman and there were numerous body scans. But to everyone's relief, all went well, and the results proved that there was no cause for concern – or was there? Jonah was left with a real and serious worry . . . was he, he wondered, running the risk of being contaminated with radiation fallout from all those X-rays?

In common with many of the stories surrounding Barrington, this may sound too far-fetched to be true. But

5

when judged by conventional standards, the man *is* somewhat eccentric. Nevertheless, he is also highly articulate and the theory and psychology behind both his training schedule and his lifestyle appear totally logical when explained in detail. He is also quite capable of directing his sense of humour against himself. He once referred to his '71st comeback' and, on another occasion, he was so annoyed to find himself placed in what he considered to be a lowly position in the world rankings that he threatened to play on until his contemporaries passed away one by one and thus he achieved his rightful place above them!

His television coaching programmes clearly illustrate his infectious enthusiasm. The sight of Barrington on court with a young teenager and a grey-haired veteran springs to mind: 'Here we have young Lochinvar', declared Jonah pointing to the young man, 'and he is trying to trap the Ancient Mariner. The back of the court is his graveyard.'

With his best days as a player now past, his attention has turned increasingly towards coaching and the promotion of the game. In 1979, he coached the British amateur team to an amazing victory in the World Championships in Australia. David Davies, chief sports writer for *The Birmingham Post*, in his sports review of the year, recalled Barrington's frustration at the fact that this achievement had not been given more publicity: 'Late in October, the sports' editor was on the receiving end of an enthusiastic telephonic blast from Jonah Barrington. "This blankety-blank Great British Amateur Squash team," declared Jonah, "has blankety well won the world title against the blankety Pakistanis, and as blankety usual, no blank has reported it." Well, the *Post*, not daring not to, promptly did; and what pleasure it gave us, too.' Perhaps it was just as well that the leading provincial newspaper did see fit to report the British triumph as Barrington had threatened to run naked around Birmingham's Bull Ring Shopping Centre in order to get the publicity which he insisted was the team's due!

More recently, Barrington has devoted more and more time to youth coaching schemes. Following his triumph with the British amateur team, it was his intention to coach the

British Open squad. But finding some of the country's leading players less than enthusiastic about his methods, he decided instead to embark on an ambitious youth coaching programme ranging down even to an Under-10 national squad. His aim? To make Britain the strongest squash nation in the world by 1990 and to produce a future British world champion. In some quarters, however, fears were expressed and a number of parents trembled at the thought of a fitness fanatic like Barrington getting his hands on their poor little kids. But the youngsters on these courses would appear to have enjoyed themselves hugely and to have suffered no permanent damage at the hands of the man they have nicknamed 'Jaws' and 'Captain Beaky'.

The Jonah Barrington story is a classic example of what one man can achieve through sheer willpower. His training methods show just how much a sportsman can extract from his body. Through the repeated breaking of pain barriers, he achieved a level of fitness that, allied with his ability, has made him a sporting legend. It was Barrington who was largely instrumental in creating a totally new attitude to fitness that now sees middle-aged businessmen all over the country opting out of the soft life for a few hours each week in order to chase around a squash court.

Quite what lies ahead for the game in general and Barrington in particular is difficult to predict. Squash after all has considerable limitations as a major spectator sport. But Barrington still has his own visions of the mountains he must climb. The Squash Rackets Association has put him in charge of what it considers to be an élite coaching programme, and it is his firm belief that the 1980s will produce another squash boom in this country through television and coaching programmes. In fact he does not consider that what happened in the 1970s ever constituted a major boom despite the massive impact made by the sport with relatively little media coverage. 'What happened was just a minor explosion compared with what is to come', he insists. It is difficult to see such a forceful personality disappearing into obscurity.

2. The Major's Son

Quite why Major Charles Barrington chose to move to the rugged, remote parish of Morwenstow in the north-east corner of Cornwall remains something of a mystery. But in 1938 the retired army officer bought an interesting country house there, with five acres of grounds, known as Marratons. The property sat by a winding country road on a hill that dropped down into the little hamlet of Woodford, and here Major Barrington was to remain for the rest of his life, bringing up his family on a modest private income. His third child – Jonah Paul Barrington – was born on 29 April 1941 at Stratton Hospital and named after Sir Jonah Barrington, the nineteenth-century Irish politician best remembered for his book, *The Irish Nation*, an evocative portrait of Ireland in the early 1800s.

Jonah's theory is that his father went to Cornwall to escape the consequences of his active membership of the British Fascist Movement at a time when the darker implications of the doctrine and Adolf Hitler's ambitions of conquest were becoming disturbingly clear:

> He was very secretive about his past but one day when I was a youngster he showed me his Fascist uniform. He also told me that he was once a member of a British Fascist delegation that visited Italy. He was very impressed with the achievements of the Mussolini and Hitler and the Fascist movement.
>
> By the time he moved to Cornwall there was quite a lot of feeling in Britain against the movement and, when war broke out, he had already gone to ground to avoid any risk of reprisals. He was undoubtedly impressed with Hitler's achievements, the reorganisation of Germany, the way the war machine

had been resurrected and the way the Fuhrer had dealt with major problems such as unemployment. But at least he had the intelligence to realise the man had started to overreach himself and that, at some point, he had to be stopped.

No doubt as a legacy of his membership of the movement my father had his own secret armoury of weapons hidden in the house. My brother handed it in to the police after his death. My father didn't bother with licences. He had .38s, .45s and a sten gun. I can remember he told me once how he had brought arms into this country from Ireland, including a revolver he had managed to smuggle through customs in a cake.

The historian, Count Nikolai Tolstoy, author of *Stalin's Secret War* and *Victims of Yalta*, has been a lifelong friend of the Barrington family. He recalls how, after the Second World War had ended, Charles Barrington would reminisce with him about the days when he had been a supporter of the Fascist movement:

I have a feeling that he was with a rival group to Mosley's Fascists but the moment war was declared, he went into his backyard and solemnly burnt his blackshirt and all the Fascist literature he had collected. Soon afterwards he received a letter from the Home Office appointing him head of the local Home Guard and, as such, he was able to get up to all sorts of Dad's Army tricks, which he enjoyed hugely.

He was a very intelligent, well-read man and something of a romantic. I don't think he had any ideological commitment to Fascism despite the fact that he had visited Italy and had many books about Italian Fascism. He also had what today would be regarded as some rather offensive Fascist stickers, the type of thing they used to put on telephone boxes. But what really appealed to him was the movement's soldier-of-fortune element. He wasn't at all in the mould of some people who, clutching their third

brandy, snarl, 'What this country needs is a dose of
what Mussolini gave Italy'.

I once asked him what he did as an active member
of the movement and he looked a bit awkward. He
told me that in Carlisle – I don't know why or when he
was there – he had a Fascist cell of several hundred
railway workers. 'You must have had popular
appeal,' I remarked. 'Whatever did you do with
them?' 'Well,' he said, 'we used to have damned good
suppers and sing-songs.'

He also kept a number of weapons in a secret room
behind his study. It wasn't that secret really because
you could see the keyhole in the bookcase. It was a
tiny room full of rifles and revolvers, including a
beautiful Luger with replaceable barrels, all in working order and preserved in oil in tin boxes. There
were also bayonets and swords and he claimed that he
had once had 80 hand grenades – presumably for the
day of the great coup – but had got rid of them
because he was frightened the two boys might find
them and pull the pins out. He also had records of
Nazi music, bought from Germany before the war –
very stirring marches. Very late at night, when we
would be laughing and talking, he would put these on
the gramophone full blast and march around the
room. Kathleen Barrington hated them and would
bang on the floor trying to get her husband to take
them off.

A few years ago, I was browsing through a history
of British Fascism and out of curiosity I looked in the
index. There was the name of Charles Barrington.
There was only a brief mention of him in the book,
something to the effect that he was one of the most
notorious leaders of Fascism in the West Country. I
remember thinking that if this is history, no wonder
people think it's bunk.

For whatever reasons Major Barrington descended on
Cornwall, Morwenstow was to provide a very happy home
for his family. He and his second wife, Kathleen, had pro-

duced their first child, Geraldine, in 1936 when they were living in Herefordshire. Soon after their arrival in Cornwall in 1939, their first son, Nicholas, was born, followed by Jonah two years later. Jonah's first memory is a vague recollection of being pushed by the family nanny in a pram down a country lane. He also remembers the announcement of the end of the war echoing from the radio while he was in the study with his mother. When he was about five, he recalls walking with his brother and sister to a local farm and being told that a very famous man was staying there . . . the Olympic gold medallist, Harold Abrahams, whose track feats would be recaptured for millions in the 1981 award-winning film, *Chariots of Fire*. To Jonah, Abrahams seemed a very heavily-built man with a huge nose, but he was delighted to see the children and insisted on walking with them the two miles back to their home.

Marratons itself was something of a children's paradise. It was a comfortable, rambling house with a labyrinth of small rooms. A postbox is set into the gateway from which a long drive, flanked by a small wood, leads to the house itself. Close at hand stands a walled archway leading to the stable block. Beyond the five acres of unspoilt grounds lie open fields that run away to the tops of the tallest cliffs in Cornwall, cliffs that were once notorious for shipwrecks and smugglers. Spread over that rugged landscape to the north-east of the nearby town of Bude are the four small hamlets that comprise Morwenstow – Woodford, set a short distance down the hill from Marratons, Shop, Gooseham and Crosstown where you can find The Bush Inn and, a little further away, above an inlet, the parish church of St John the Baptist.

But for a quirk of fate, the philosopher Bertrand Russell might well have become the owner of Marratons instead of the Barringtons. Geraldine Barrington still has a letter from the writer Gerald Brennan after he had visited the house in the late 1930s and viewed it as a possible home on behalf of Russell and his third wife, Patricia Spence:

It is a very rambling but compact house with great character of its own. I should say it was 15th century with lots of alterations made to it. It is in excellent condition . . . and has had a good deal of money spent on it to make it a gentleman's residence. The rooms were pretty, the only disadvantage being that the lower rooms seem dark. The ceilings are rather low . . . The electric light engine was a modern foolproof one and the owner said it had never given him any trouble.

The stables, garages etc . . . are large buildings. The house is entirely surrounded by thick woods, orchards and hedges which must keep off the wind as well as giving a feeling of privacy . . . the major has not allowed any trees to be pruned for 10 years. Apple trees, fuchsias and beeches combine to form a sort of jungle which is most romantic. The house is run with one servant and one gardener. All the local tradesmen, a dozen at least, call regularly. There is a postbox at the end of the drive – one post in and one post out every day.

I jot these things as I think of them. I certainly think the house might suit you very well and strongly advise you to come and see it. By the way, the owner seems an honest man and pointed out the defects most conscientiously . . . Morwena, founder of the church of Morwenstow in the sixth century, is the patron saint of Irish mathematics, apparently the little has been preserved of them . . . she came here, converted the heathen and founded a school where they were taught the principles of Euclid and how to tie very complicated knots. Recently her well has dried up but I have no doubt if Bertie comes to live in her parish, it will run with water again.

The Russells, however, never managed to see the house and so they didn't buy it. A thick mist came down as they were trying to find it and they turned back!

To this day Marratons remains unspoilt and is accessible only by negotiating a bewildering maze of narrow country lanes. Those lanes baffled at least one young man invited to visit Major and Mrs Barrington's strikingly attractive daughter. 'I can remember one of Geraldine's boyfriends arriving at some unearthly hour of the night,' recalls Jonah. 'He had spent two hours trying to find the house and all the time he had been within a mile of the place.'

The property is still owned by the Barringtons and each morning Edna Brown, who has worked for the family since 1948, cleans the house even though it remains empty for much of the year. In the summer, certain parts may be let to guests, and two or three times a year Geraldine herself returns from London to the peace of Marratons with her husband, merchant banker Anthony Richmond-Watson, and their family.

The house has changed little since Jonah was a boy. The extension built by Major Barrington took away that darkness in those lower rooms referred to by Gerald Brennan in his letter. Perhaps the Major's train set and vast army of toy soldiers have been sold, but his library remains intact with endless volumes about his great hero, Napoleon, and about Irish history, including Sir Jonah Barrington's book *The Irish Nation*, standing on a bookshelf only a few yards away from his portrait hanging in the hall. One or two books on Fascism that presumably survived that bonfire remain – Aline Lion's *The Pedigree of Fascism* and *The Fascist Movement* by Luigi Villari, with passages that struck the Major as important underlined in pencil. Occasionally one comes across a book such as *The Inimitable Jeeves* by P.G. Wodehouse, evidence that illustrates the lighter side of the retired army officer's character. Everywhere on the ground floor are drawings and ornaments which indicate that this was the house of a military man. And a massive pre-war Aga cooker dominates the tiny kitchen where once the Barringtons assembled for their afternoon tea.

As Jonah and his elder brother, Nicholas, grew up, an intense rivalry developed between them. Jonah forever struggled to compete with the large gangling boy who proved talented both inside the classroom and on the sports field and who also had the distinct advantage of being two years older. The two boys fought endlessly, as all boys do, but fortunately the fights never developed to a serious stage because Nick was always able to control Jonah at will, either by putting his head in an armlock or simply by sitting on top of him. Throughout the year endless games of cricket or football would be played in the garden, as the dogs ran around, barking in the fun. Often village friends such as the Tape brothers, David and Tony, would join in. And when *Dick Barton* came on the radio, Jonah would be left frantically trying to find a way to get into the house after Nick had locked him out. On one occasion, Jonah was so furious at his exclusion from a particularly crucial episode that he smashed the glass in the back door with his bare fist, cutting himself in the process so severely that he carries the scars to this day.

A mile or so along the narrow country lanes is the small school of St Mark's in the village of Shop where the two boys had their first taste of education. Jonah remembers a rather fierce, elderly schoolmistress who achieved some impressive results by resorting to levels of violence that would hardly be fashionable today: 'Whenever you got a sum wrong, she would swipe you across the ear. A boy called Philip Staddon, who later became an executive with Shell, and I used to work together tactically. What we would do was get Donald Branton, who later became a doctor, to go up to the front of the class to be marked first because he was invariably the boy who got hit. When he returned to the desk alongside us, we copied down the answers he had got right and tried to find different answers for the ones he had got wrong!'

Jonah's village childhood remains vividly in his memory as an intensely happy period of his life. Too young to remember the war years and living in a part of the world that escaped the ravages of the Blitz, his early memories are of a father who was a remarkable character, a mother who manipulated her household expertly and an environment where he had no choice but to develop his competitive instincts, simply to survive against his brother:

In the morning, mother was totally in control. When it came to the evening, my old man came into his own, only fading around 3 am! In his own way, he had an enormous amount of self-discipline. His breakfast

14

had to arrive at the same time every morning about 11.30 and exactly the same thing was always on the tray . . . the egg had to have been boiled for precisely the right period of time otherwise it would be sent back immediately. In his last few years, he always drank squeezed lemon juice because someone in the parish had told him it was the secret of old age.

My father's parents lived in Liverpool. Mother was the daughter of a master mariner and had been born at sea. Father went to Sandhurst and served with the 13th Hussars in the First World War fighting against the Turks in Mesopotamia. After the war, he was posted to Dublin during the Irish Civil War. He was involved in the conflict but in what way he never really told me. He was an ardent Protestant, not that he went to church regularly, but in his antipathy to Catholicism. At the same time, he loved Ireland and at heart was a fervent Irish nationalist. He tried hard to believe in a united Ireland but didn't want any connection with a load of papists. It was very strange. Obviously a united Ireland would never have had a Protestant government. But he had a great sense of humour and I am sure he would have chuckled to himself about the inconsistency of his viewpoint. He was a small man, only about 5ft 7in tall and also very neat; his hair was always immaculately brushed. While Nick and I were devoted to sport, he would spend a good part of the day absorbed in his books or working in the garden if it was summer.

Without doubt father was an eccentric – but a great conversationalist and very popular in the village. He never worked after leaving the army because he was able to survive on his independent income. His family had owned a glass factory in Liverpool and they made a lot of money when it was sold. He may not have gone off to work in the morning like most fathers, but he never wasted a single moment of the day once he had got up. He was always there when we needed him. I suppose he regarded himself as something of a warrior-historian. During the war, he was put in charge of the local Home Guard and he would always hold his drilling parades near The Bush Inn so the lads could go straight into the pub afterwards. He was deadly with a rifle – locally they used to talk about the day Major Barrington put a bullet through two rabbits with the same shot. Our neighbour, Captain Clifford Saxton, was a great friend of his but while Dad was Chairman of the local Conservative Association, Saxton was an avowed Liberal. They would argue about anything. One night 'Sack', as we called him, and my father had a terrible row. My old man dashed into his armoury and, five minutes later, they were shooting at each other.

Nicholas also recalls this story:

Without a doubt they were firing at each other, both no doubt under the influence of alcohol; mother and Mrs Saxton were on the phone during the hostilities asking each other what the hell to do. But neither of them was hurt and they were really the greatest of friends. If they had been out shooting together and the day had not gone well, they would take pot shots at the postbox by the village hall from the other side of the green. Not the sort of thing you do now but they were living in a different age then. People just thought, 'Oh there go Major Barrington and Captain Saxton enjoying themselves.'

Further evidence of Major Barrington's eccentricity lay in the fact that he devoted quite a considerable time to playing with his model railway. 'One Christmas', recalls Jonah, 'he bought us a circular track and a train. It was a present for my brother and me but we were never allowed to use it. He would blow the train whistle while the engine was going full tilt at two in the morning and mother would bang on the floor to get him to stop.'

Apart from Sunday lunch, mealtimes at Marratons were invariably held without the head of the household, for Major Barrington would eat by himself in the lounge. But when afternoon tea was taken he would always be found with the rest of the family in the small kitchen and there he would gaze out of the window at his garden drinking very weak tea with enormous amounts of sugar and eating thin slices of brown bread covered with Gentleman's Relish.

Barrington's mother, Kathleen, who took great pride in her claim that she was descended from the Welsh Princes, was therefore left to cope with the realities of life – realities that in later years were to become an increasing problem as the independent means that had allowed the major to live the life of a country gentleman began to dwindle. 'Mother was an expert at manipulating bills,' says Jonah. 'She never paid one in full. If a bill was £60, she would pay £5 and that would keep them quiet. My father didn't want to know, he would just bury his head in the sand. In later years, he even took a job delivering groceries for the local shopkeeper but the problem was he loved talking to people and spent too much time in The Bush Inn. So those deliveries would sometimes arrive as late as one or two in the morning.'

At an early age, Count Nikolai Tolstoy came to know the Barringtons well. As a young boy, his father had escaped to England, leaving his grandfather in Russia fighting for the White Army against the Reds. When he arrived he joined his great-aunt, who was staying at Bude Castle as a guest of Admiral Sir Douglas Nicholson, who had been commander of the Home Fleet during the First World War. His father soon married a Devon girl from the nearby village of Apple-dore, and Nikolai was born in 1935:

> My father loved walking around Morwenstow and he took my sister and me there for a holiday at a farm called Stanbury. During that visit we met the Barringtons. They would have guests at Marratons and, during the summer of 1947, we went there for a month's holiday. I remember we had to travel in the back of a lorry because of the petrol shortage.

Count Tolstoy has not forgotten his first meeting with the younger Barrington son:

Jonah wore very long shorts with braces holding them up outside his shirt and looked like a cheerful ragamuffin. He was very lively and amusing. I will never forget him jumping up and down on a chair with his little legs barely reaching the floor continually singing 'I AM THE GREATEST MAN IN THE WORLD.' I think from the beginning he decided he would be the greatest one way or another.

Although Tolstoy was only eleven or twelve when he first met Major Barrington, they got on terribly well. The young boy's fascination with history, springing from his family's involvement in the epic events that transformed Russia, appealed strongly to the former soldier. While his own sons were more interested in kicking a football around or wielding a cricket bat outside, here was a boy who really appreciated the hundreds of history books that lined the Major's shelves, who loved to hear him reminisce about the First World War and the Irish troubles. Despite the age gap, the young count and the ex-army officer developed a great friendship. 'We had so much in common and in some respects he always remained a schoolboy at heart with his love of adventure,' says Count Tolstoy:

When I was older and visited Marratons, he would pull out a bottle of Irish whisky and we would talk for hours about Napoleon, Cromwell and various other historical subjects. He told me that, during the First World War, he had taken part in one of the last cavalry charges ever to be made by the British army, and after they had cut through a Turkish infantry column with swords drawn, they turned around and cut through their ranks for a second time. I still have a Russian rifle he gave me that he had retrieved from a Turk who had in turn got it from a Cossack.

After the war, he went to Dublin taking a Persian manservant called Akbar with him. My understanding was that he served with the British army in the Irish troubles and later with the Free State Army against the IRA. He had a scar right across his side that I believe he acquired when he was shot by an IRA gunman on a bus. Those were dangerous times. Another story he told me was that, one night, when he was at the theatre in Dublin, having a drink in the foyer during the interval, all the lights suddenly went out due to an electricity failure. When they came back on again, nearly everybody in the room had drawn their guns and were putting them away again rather sheepishly. He led what he described as a rake-hell bachelor existence in Dublin before he married his first wife. She died later at a young age. Why he went to England I don't know.

As well as his armoury, he had the most marvellous collection of toy soldiers. There were about 3,000 of them but he never got them all out for me because there were so many. He worshipped Napoleon and the extraordinary thing about this was that his squadron was called upon for special duty to provide the military escort for the funeral of Empress Eugénie, the widow of Napoleon III. Out of all the men in the army, they picked the man who worshipped Napoleon and was obsessed by everything connected with the family.

He had a great sense of humour, which his family – particularly Jonah – inherited. Another wonderful thing about the Barringtons was that, despite all the arguments, and there were many, all would be forgotten and forgiven the next day. It was a very happy home. There'd be shouting and screaming, guns would be brandished and even fired, but the next morning it was as if nothing had ever happened. Once Jonah and I were drinking with his father when an argument flared up. The Major said he had had enough of us two boys, opened up his secret armoury, got out a Luger and loaded it. He went back into the dining room and sat down to eat his supper with a glass of whisky by his side, saying: 'If either of those two boys pass the hall door, I swear I'll put a bullet through them.' Fortunately you could get around Marratons without having to pass that particular door!

There is no doubt that Jonah inherited many of his father's characteristics – his love of conversation, his ability to talk for hours, a rebellious streak, his deep affection for Ireland and the Irish people and his lack of concern for everyday money matters. Like his father, he has always had a point of view and is never afraid to express it and, like his father, he, too, came to be viewed as somewhat eccentric in later life. Indeed, all three Barrington children inherited their parents' ability to appreciate the funny side of life. Asked not long ago what he thought of his famous brother, Nick Barrington replied: 'I am immensely proud of Jonah but I don't want him to buy the house next door to me. He might have me out running.' Did Jonah change after he became world champion? 'Yes, he became even less punctual!' Count Tolstoy says that when Jonah is laughing, he has the look of his father on his face. But it was from his mother, too, who was well capable of holding her own in the Major's company, that Jonah inherited his ability to find irony and humour in the most serious situations. From her, also, he acquired that strength of character which, with his father's individuality, would provide a remarkable combination in later life.

3. Schooldays

The idyllic existence enjoyed by the two Barrington boys in
Morwenstow came to an end in 1950 when Major
Barrington decided to send them away to boarding school.
His choice was Headfort, a recently opened Irish prepara-
tory school in Kells, Co. Meath, some forty miles north of
Dublin. No doubt his great love of Ireland was his main
reason but he was also somewhat disturbed that his sons
were developing pronounced Cornish accents, and that
simply would not do.

At first Jonah resented leaving the village and his friends
at the age of nine. Nevertheless, once he had adjusted to
the change, he was to have a marvellous five years at
Headfort. The journey to the Irish school was in itself
something of an epic. After travelling the eight miles to
Bude, a train journey followed to London where a master
always met the English boys who were pupils at the school.
Then he conducted them by train across country and then
over the sea to Ireland. Nick well remembers the mock
fights he and Jonah staged at each station so that they could
keep a compartment to themselves.

Jonah was very happy during his five years at prep
school. Lord and Lady Headfort had started the school at
their Georgian country mansion in order to make some
money. The house was surrounded by an enormous estate
with the Blackwater River running through it. In the middle
of the river was a bridge leading onto a forested island full
of huge bushes where the boys would be taken now and
again to play cowboys and Indians. It was a marvellous
environment for a young lad:

I was exceedingly lucky at Headfort because I ran into
a master called Jack Sweetman. Without realising it at

21

the time, he was to be a major influence on my life. A wonderful sportsman, he played both rugby and cricket for Leinster province and also soccer for Swindon Town in the Combination League. He was an exceptional rugby player, a stocky back-row forward who had been a wartime reserve for the Irish team. Many considered him unlucky not to have been capped by his country. What impressed me so much was his discipline. He was my idea of a top-class sportsman. He trained regularly, he didn't drink, he didn't smoke. He was also an outstanding teacher. I loved soccer but I began to enjoy rugby, too. Had it been taught by someone else, I don't think that would have happened. Besides my father, two men played the most powerful roles in my development. The first was Jack Sweetman and the second was my coach, Nasrullah Khan. But Jack Sweetman's influence was just as great as Naz's. My attitude to squash, my instinctive acceptance of the disciplines imposed on me later by Naz, were possible because of Jack Sweetman.

Young Barrington proved to be a star pupil at Headfort. He became head of the school, he captained the school at rugby, cricket and hockey. His highly competitive instincts, so evident in his early rivalry with Nick at Morwenstow, were soon apparent at Headfort. 'I won the school rugby-ball kicking competition when no one expected me to and then the following year when I was expected to win, I didn't, and threw a real tantrum. I also remember playing in the final of the school tennis tournament with my brother and going up to the headmaster, David Wild, and demanding that there should be some kind of prize. And even after he had explained kindly that tennis was amateur sport like the Olympics, I still insisted: "But even in the Olympics they get medals".'

Jonah also remembers receiving six of the best after being caught reciting some ribald poetry, a rather crude version of 'Old Mother Riley Had A Cow', *et al.*, to the other boys in

22

his dormitory after lights-out. But crimes such as this were mild in comparison with those of another pupil known as Trapper Jessel, a gifted athlete not averse to exercising his dominance over the other boys: 'He was a horrendous bully. I remember he used to make one boy drink ink. When he left, he made sure there was a collection for him as he said he was sure we loved him so much! Later I heard that he had gone to St Columba's, the public school near Dublin, and had been thrown out for making a bomb which he rolled down a hill at some school building.'

At Headfort, Jonah became a great friend of one of his contemporaries, Michael Chamberlayne, whose nickname was 'Polly' because his blond hair tended to stick up to such an extent that he bore a vague resemblance to a parrot. His home was the family farm at Chamberlainstown, just four miles from the school, and there Barrington also met Polly's sister, Pauline, known for some reason as Pilly. She remembers two Jonahs – the one at Headfort and, later, the one at Trinity College, Dublin. The prep school Jonah she remembers as something of a star pupil: 'He was the masters' favourite because he was brilliant at everything. He was such a good sportsman and he was very clever too.'

It may be almost thirty years since Barrington was at Headfort but Jack Sweetman, now the senior master at the school, still has vivid recollections of the small, dark-haired, good-looking boy:

Jonah might have been small but he was a jolly good sportsman. He could have been a very fine rugby player if he had continued playing the game, certainly a first-class player. He was a very good kicker, he had very good hands and he was a tricky runner with the ability to sidestep and swerve. He had a very alert mind, was fast over a short distance and reacted quickly to any situation. I remember him playing against a Dublin school and scoring in every possible way, a try, a dropped goal, a penalty and a conversion. He was a natural sportsman. I don't think there was any doubt that he was better than his brother Nick as he was much more nimble on his feet.

Jonah and Nick would address each other as 'brother' during their not infrequent arguments. Jonah would often challenge statements, and no one could hope to get away with a careless remark when he was around. All this probably had much to do with the articulate Barrington the world came to know.

David Wild, now living in retirement in an attractive country house on the edge of Dartmoor, pointed to his sofa and cast his mind back to the day when the two Barrington boys, dressed in white shirts and white shorts, were seated there shortly after he had become headmaster of Headfort:

Major Barrington and his wife had brought the boys in to see me. I was puzzled that they wanted to send them to Ireland but Mrs Barrington told me that they were thinking of following their sons out after a while, though of course they never did. The Major semed a drifty sort of person and it struck me as strange that the mother seemed to be making the important family decisions. They turned out to be two very gifted boys, intellectually as well as athletically. Jonah, of course, was very able, but he didn't have quite the same drive as Nicky in the classroom. This was probably because he found his work easy. He was very fluent and if he was writing an essay, he would cover the subject with great confidence. And he passed out top of the Common Entrance list.

Yes, Jonah was small for his age, but he was one of the most gifted fly-halves I ever saw in my career at Headfort. If the ball was anywhere near him, he would never drop it. He had wonderful confidence and he was very fortunate we had such a very good games master in Jack Sweetman. I can remember in one school match we were either a few points down or the scores were level, very near the final whistle. The ball was passed to Jonah and he dropped a goal to win the match. Very few other boys would have had that sort of confidence. They would have passed the ball out so that the wing could try to score. I remember

24

Jack saying afterwards, 'That boy might go the whole way.' He was also a good cricketer. We had a squash court at Headfort, which was unusual for a prep school, where Nicky and I used to play because we were about the same standard. The funny thing was that Jonah wasn't at all keen on squash then.

When David Wild retired in 1974, he was both surprised and honoured that Jonah, with his wife, Madeline, returned for his farewell party, having flown over specially from Sweden. 'I was astonished – it was a great compliment to me. I lost count how many times he ran around the playing fields the next morning!' David Wild was also rather surprised at what happened to Barrington later. 'I don't know where he found his extraordinary self-discipline after what had happened at university. It didn't fit in with his childhood where everything came so easily. He would make the effort but I would never have expected the sort of concentration he later showed in his squash career. Had he showed that sort of determination at Headfort he would undoubtedly have got a scholarship to Cheltenham.'

The prep school sporting hero was to find life rather different when he did go to Cheltenham College, the famous public school in the attractive Regency Spa town well known for its Gold Cup race meeting. Past members of the Barrington family had been to Cheltenham, as had David Wild, and Jonah found it altogether harder to make his mark as a sportsman in competition with some 450 other pupils, despite the good reports that preceded him from Headfort:

At that stage, the only thing I was really interested in was sport. I always remember my first game of rugby at Cheltenham. It was some sort of house trial and I played for a side that was steamrollered by the opposition. So as far as those running the game were concerned, I was a loser and put on the sideboard. I knew that rugby was a game for which I had a lot of ability. But I had no control whatever over what was happening and because of that one single trial, I became more and more insular and more and more inhibited.

There were other factors, too, that turned Barrington into an unhappy pupil at Cheltenham. He was put in a stream with boys who had already been at the school for a year and, as the smallest boy in the class, he became even more aware of his inferior size. He felt that those boys who had come to Cheltenham by way of the Junior School had a distinct advantage over outsiders. Furthermore, when he arrived, he was put in a waiting house until there was room in the house to which he had originally been allotted. All this conspired to unsettle him even before he had to face what he considered to be the horrors of the College Combined Cadet Force:

Once a week we went through the business of dressing up in an appalling uniform and being marched around by little dictators. They bawled you out and gave you extra duties, which I detested. The uniform was like a big hairshirt. I had found I had a skin reaction to certain coarse cloths – my mother always had a problem getting the right kind of material for my trousers. Those extraordinary corps trousers I had to wear couldn't have been worse. I used the pyjama trick. At first I thought there was something wrong with me but then I discovered that probably half the school was disappearing into the loo to put their pyjamas on before going out to do corps!

Having been Head of School at Headfort and captain of every sport before coming to Cheltenham, where I was a small fish in a now much bigger pool, was an experience I found hard to take. From the very free existence at Headfort I suddenly found myself at a school where the discipline was totally different – what I would call mindless discipline. You had to do things you instinctively thought were not logical.

Just before Jonah's fourteenth birthday, another trauma added still further to his misery. 'I was quite a reasonable

26

cricketer but one day I remember playing and being totally unable to do anything but stonewall. I couldn't see anything until the ball was right on top of me. I also recall sitting in a classroom – one minute I could see what was written on the blackboard quite clearly and then it would all go wavy. I had always made fun of my brother because he was so short-sighted. He had a fundamental weakness with his eyes and suddenly I had the same problem. I had become short-sighted. I needed glasses and I hated it.'

Taken in isolation, each of these experiences might have been manageable, but to such a highly sensitive and intelligent fourteen-year-old, what seemed like an endless succession of traumatic problems proved to be more than he could cope with. He became increasingly miserable and disturbed until the inevitable day when everything exploded and the young Jonah Barrington suffered a most unusual experience for a schoolboy – a nervous breakdown.

In the terminology of the day, you could say I had a crack-up. I just couldn't stand it any longer. I was having perpetual nightmares and I think I scared the daylights out of everybody in my dormitory. My father promptly closed his mind to the whole episode, so it was left to my mother to come up to Cheltenham. I was promptly carted off to a shrink. He got out lots of coloured cubes and asked me endless questions. If he said white, I was meant to say black and so on. This went on for about half-an-hour and then he took my mother to one side and boldly pronounced his opinion that I had a mental age of about nine! Naturally enough, his diagnosis appalled my mother, who took me post-haste back to Cornwall to stay with a psychologist called Forbes-Dennis in St. Ives. He was married to the novelist Phyllis Bottome and they were both very kind to me and must have been some help as the nightmares stopped and I began to feel less strung-up. They had a little kitten called Willow and I used to run around their garden playing with it. Forbes-Dennis used to analyse my dreams and question me about them. I just used to

27

make up anything that came into my mind, be-
lieving I was one jump ahead of him but he was
probably a step ahead of me, working out the
significance of everything I told him whether it was
true or not.

In the opinion of Jonah's sister Geraldine, his upbringing
probably contributed greatly to the breakdown: 'Thinking
back, we had all led a sheltered life and Jonah, being the
youngest, had had a lot of things done for him. He couldn't
even tie his tie before he went away to Headfort. When he
got to Cheltenham, he had to start all over again and in a
much larger school. I don't think it would have been any
different if he had gone somewhere else. He just didn't
adapt. I remember how upset we all were. One simply
didn't know anyone who had had a nervous breakdown:
one never even thought about it.'

Elder brother Nicholas had never really taken much
notice of Jonah at Cheltenham. The strictly defined strata
of seniority between public schoolboys simply did not
permit such a thing. 'I never noticed any breakdown,' he
recalls dismissively. 'I've always been sceptical of anyone
who has a breakdown. It's normally an effort to avoid one's
responsibilities. Without doubt, Jonah's problem was that
he had been a rather important fish in a small pond at
Headfort and then suddenly he became a tiny fish in an
enormous ocean. Jonah did have another disadvantage I
suppose, being physically small; at the age of thirteen or
fourteen, size can make a big difference.'

Before too long, Jonah was pronounced fit enough to
return to Cheltenham where matters did in fact improve to
some degree. Nevertheless, to this day, he is still unable to
regard his time there as anything other than the worst
period of his life. In his own words, Humpty Dumpty had
come down with a great fall. Maybe nobody attempted to
put the pieces together again at Cheltenham but, in a
gradual and still painful process, he was to achieve some
measure of sporting recognition and, eventually, the
academic talents which had been carefully nurtured and
developed at Headfort were to surface.

It was following his nervous breakdown that Barrington was to take his first genuine interest in the game that was to form such an all-important part of his future life. Two hundred yards from the house to which he was at last sent, and of which he had waited so long to become an integral member, were the College's four squash courts. With their low ceilings and concrete floors, however, they were never allowed to be used for individual competition, as the benefactor who had originally donated them had insisted that such self-seeking was undesirable in public school men! Competition should be strictly limited to inter-school team matches. Consequently, Cheltenham's individual squash competitions had to be conducted at Major Ted Millman's Owe 40 club where the former army major, now a professional squash and tennis coach, literally held court. Here the young Barrington was given his first squash lesson. 'Jooonaah', roared the major in archetypal Sandhurst tones, 'look alive, me boy, we're gooing to enjooy a jolly scaampaah!'

Jonah will never forget those exciting days. 'The club had a bar and Major Millman, when he wasn't scampering around the court, wasn't averse to us having a beer there. Sheila Speight, who, as Mrs Macintosh, won the 1960 British Championship, also played at the club and my brother, who was then a much better player than I was, once underwent the fearful shock of being beaten by this formidable lady. I really enjoyed squash in my final year. It was basically a minor sport but at Cheltenham we had some very fine players. A boy called Medway, known as Dimmers because his initials were D.I.M., was ranked as the second best schoolboy in Britain. He was older than I was but, as we were in the same house, we would sometimes have a game together. I became very heated and exceptionally angry with myself on one occasion because he was beating me so easily and I just didn't seem able to do any better. I spat on the floor with rage and a shocked Dimmers immediately called me "A vile child" and refused to continue the game. So off I went, taking my ball with me, leaving him open-mouthed behind me. There was no way he was going to have the last word!'

By the time Barrington was a member of the Cheltenham College team, both Dimmers and Nicholas had left. Initially, Jonah played third string behind a boy called Conway-Gordon and also Chris Williams, who was sadly to meet a tragically early death as a racing driver. In *The Gloucestershire Echo* of 20 March 1958, a back page headline declared COLLEGE TEAM AGAIN UNBEATEN. Beneath it was a report of the College's 3–0 victory against Wrekin which completed a second successive season without defeat. 'After the match', said the report, 'colours were awarded to G. Conway-Gordon and J. Barrington, neither of whom has lost a game in school matches this year. A feature of the match was Barrington's accuracy on the drop-volley . . .'

Jonah's membership of the squash squad involved a visit to Paris in 1958. 'We were billetted on various local families', he remembers, 'and early one afternoon, the lady of the house we were staying in banged loudly on the door of our room protesting, "Don't you want to see the Eiffel Tower? Don't you even want to see Notre Dame?" Some obscenity was muttered in response and she rapidly departed in shocked silence. Little did she know that we had been investigating the fleshpots of Montmartre until seven o'clock that very morning and were not really in any mood for sightseeing. There had been a certain amount of consorting with the ladies of the town – it was all very educational!'

The school team played the Jeu de Paume et de Rackets Club, losing the first match 3–1 and drawing the second 2–2, with Barrington, at No 3, being the only player to win both his matches. By coincidence, Dimmers, now in France and reputedly the country's leading player, was a member of the French club and, in the first match, beat Chris Williams 9–1, 9–7 and 9–6. 'It was very much the old style privileged rackets and real tennis club of Paris,' recalls Jonah. 'The club itself, in the Rue Lauriston, had apparently been a Gestapo centre during the Second World War. We all had a vivid sense of the awful things that must have taken place there. The courts had shiny, slippery floors and in my vivid imagination I could see them running with blood.'

Back at Cheltenham, earlier that season, Jonah had reached the semi-finals of the town's first-ever junior squash tournament at the Owe 40 club. Players from the College team dominated the event and, after Chris Williams had beaten Barrington in the semi-finals 5–9, 9–6, 9–4, 9–2, he was himself defeated in the final by Conway-Gordon 9–5, 6–9, 4–9, 3–9. Major Millman, who had organised the event, noted afterwards: 'I am quite sure that both finalists have an excellent future in the game.' There was no mention, however, of that other college player, Barrington.

In his later year at Cheltenham, Barrington was also to reveal occasional glimpses of the other sporting talents for which he had been noted at Headfort – notably tennis and hockey. He was an important member of the tennis team until he was dropped for swearing in a school match. And on the hockey field he clearly showed what might have been when he helped his side to victory in the inter-house competition. 'I remember in one of those matches – I think it was the final – I put four or five goals past the school goalkeeper, no less. A few people were astonished including Peter Gale, our hockey master, who had played for England a few times. We crucified that other team but unfortunately it was virtually the last match I played and success came too late for me to be a contender for what might have been a place in the school team.'

There was another important factor that helped Jonah to settle back into life at Cheltenham after the disastrous start to his public-school career. His sister Geraldine was studying at a local secretarial college. 'Father wouldn't hear of her going to wicked old London' says Jonah,

and Cheltenham was something of a compromise. Little did my parents know that the town was then reputed to have the highest illegitimacy rate in the country! Before long, I discovered that she had a boyfriend at College, which appalled Nick as such a thing was totally out of order. At that time, he refused to have anything to do with girls in general and Geraldine in particular, apart from the fact that he was quick to criticise her appearance and her choice of friends. But I found her presence in the town a great solace and used to look forward to meeting up with her and the other girls from the secretarial college.

As time went by, I suppose things did get better for me at Cheltenham, even though I was still longing for the day when I could walk out of the place a free man. I wasn't the best squash player but I really enjoyed the game. I also began to do moderately well academically, perhaps because I've always had a very good memory. I was able to recite page upon page of Tacitus by heart and, no doubt due to my father's influence, I thoroughly enjoyed history. When I was fifteen, I passed seven 'O' levels and a year or two later got 'A' levels in History, English, and also in History with Foreign Text. This last was really like doing two subjects in one as you had to study French history in the French language and Roman History in Latin. I quite surprised myself and, I suspect, most of my masters, too, by getting an extraordinarily high grade. However, mathematics always remained a mystery to me. I failed Elementary Maths at 'O' level and the school put this down to sheer laziness and lack of commitment. It was considered an essential exam for everyone and they forced me to sit the bloody thing time and time again. I think I did it five times in the end. The pass mark was 98 out of a possible 200: the first time I got 90 and the last, I managed a triumphant 12. I suppose I was just uninterested. They made me do special studying and left me with lots of dull and incomprehensible books in a classroom on my own. I just used to sneak off into town. When I popped up with good 'A' levels in the other subjects, there were a number of incredulous expressions from the masters' common room. It all went to prove what I had known all along – that maths exams were totally superficial.

Jonah's 'A' level results were enough to gain him a place at Trinity College, Dublin, the educational and spiritual home of the Barrington family and the university which the major had always favoured for his son. On account of his age – he was only just seventeen – he could have stayed on at Cheltenham for another year to sit the university scholarship. Indeed, this is what his mother had always wanted, but so determined was Jonah to excise all memory of it from his mind that he packed his bags a full week before the end of term and, with a great sense of relief, caught a train for Cornwall, never to return.

'In fact', he recalls with a smile, 'I had been invited to play in a junior county tennis tournament and had to seek permission to leave early. This was promptly refused and I was outraged. After all, I had finished my 'A' levels and there was nothing else to do. As far as I was concerned, their bloody-minded attitude just about summed up my entire Cheltenham career. So I took the greatest delight in giving my last V sign to the place and everyone in it – and within a couple of hours had packed up and gone.'

To say that he had no regrets would be untrue, for his sudden departure caused him just one minor disappointment. With other like-minded contemporaries, he had helped to formulate a number of valedictory celebrations, one of which involved stabling a well-fed and watered cow in the College's cricket scorebox. Perhaps he was fortunate to have been beyond the reach of Cheltenham's disciplinary system when the awful discovery was eventually made.

During the leisurely train journey back to Cornwall which marked the end of his public-school career, Barrington had time to reflect and draw conclusions. To this day he has not found it necessary to modify his opinions by the smallest degree: 'My time at Cheltenham College was the unhappiest period of my youth. I found it a totally humourless place and I regret to say that it was the one period of my formative years in which I made no friends at all.'

4. Dublin and Disgrace

When Jonah Barrington arrived in Dublin towards the end of 1958 to start his university career, he found himself in a charming city that was a pleasantly provincial mixture of fine buildings, handsome Georgian squares and terraces, atmospheric backstreet pubs with the inevitable Guinness on tap, cosy little shops and, everywhere, church after church whose doors were always wide open.

In some ways it was unfortunate that Barrington came up to Trinity when he was only seventeen – and thus became the youngest student at the famous university. It was not a situation his mother had wanted – if she had had her way Jonah would no doubt have ended up at Oxford or Cambridge. But Jonah's father was doubly delighted that he was going to Trinity. It was where many past members of the Barrington family had studied, and also Count Tolstoy was already in residence, reading history.

After the unhappiness of Cheltenham, Jonah felt a tremendous sense of release in Dublin. He experienced a freedom he had never enjoyed before and he was reunited with many of the friends he had made at Headfort, such as 'Polly' Chamberlayne and David Cant (who had once claimed the unusual distinction for a prep-school cricketer of taking all ten wickets in a school match, thus producing the eye-catching local newspaper headline, CANT CAN).

The proliferation of pubs around the university provided plenty of rendezvous for the students. Added to this, Trinity was run with a casualness that would have astonished even those well acquainted with university life. A prime example of this informality came in a lecture young Barrington managed to attend at nine o'clock in the morning – not that frequent an event. Thirty-two students should have assembled before the lecturer but only four were present. Yet all 32 names were answered by the quartet. The lecturer viewed the matter philosophically, ticking off all the names before he began. Then, when a Greek student condescended to turn up some fifteen minutes late, the lecturer gazed at him in astonishment, over his spectacles, and said: 'Glory be to God. Is it yourself or your ghost that I'm seeing at the door?' It was said at Trinity you could take five or even six years over a degree course that in England would have taken only three.

For such a young and lively student, Dublin offered a golden opportunity to lead a rake's existence and Jonah was not beneath the challenge.

After the restrictions of the English public school system, university life was a marvellous experience, the atmosphere was so convivial. Perhaps one of the major problems was the abundance of pubs and my determination to get to know each of them. If I had been doing academic research into the drinking habits of Dublin I would have been a senior professor by the time I was nineteen, because I acquired a taste for Guinness and was soon averaging as many as ten pints a day, despite the fact that my allowance from my father was less than £5 a week.

David Cant and I shared a room together for a while before we had to do a moonlight flit because we didn't have the rent. I seemed to live the life of a bedouin, always moving on, or rather having to. In one of my many digs I remember coming home at about three in the morning and an hour or so later waking up in a drunken stupor. After staggering along the narrow corridor, I remember focusing my eyes hard on the lavatory seat, before tripping over the damn thing and going straight through the window. That must have sobered me up because, somehow or other, I managed to disentangle my head from the shattered glass and get back to bed. Of course, there was one hell of a row with the landlady the next morning and I had to move on yet again.

Towards the end of my time at Trinity, I can clearly recall another incident which still makes me go cold at the very thought of it. In the middle of the night I was clambering around on the roof of the ladies' hall of residence with a number of my friends. I can't speak for them but, to put it in legal language, I was clearly attempting to effect an entry. Luckily I was absolutely paralytic because I lost my footing, slid rapidly down the steep roof and disappeared over the edge of the building. I will always have cause to be grateful to Mr Guinness for I remained totally relaxed – I remember picking myself up from the street below and walking home, fully intending to have another go the next night.

When I arrived at Trinity, I didn't have any idea what I was going to read. Alan Jones, another of my Headfort friends, suggested that I might like to try legal science and so, in the absence of any other suggestions, I did. Before long, however, I came to the conclusion that Roman law bored me stiff, and my attendance at lectures became less and less frequent. After a while, it was obvious even to my tutor that I was paying very little attention to the curriculum and so it was suggested that I might care to have a go at history. Now while this was a subject I had always enjoyed, I found myself totally out of the habit of disciplined study and I believe a certain amount of study is rather important if you want to pass exams.

At the end of my first year, I walked out of the examination hall after dramatically tearing up my papers – rather a pathetic gesture really. But even before this, the academic staff were not unaware of my reluctance to study, a fact which came home to me rather abruptly when I was talking to one of my lecturers in Parliament Square. A filling from one of my teeth had obviously worked loose because it fell out and hit the cobblestones. The lecturer stared at me for a moment and then remarked: 'Mr Barrington, I've always thought things were going badly for you here but now you're positively disintegrating before my very eyes.'

This rather disgracing conclusion to my university career seems, in retrospect, to have caused me little shame for I attended Trinity's degree celebrations at the end of that term with a bag of flour secreted about my person. At the very moment when a Nigerian friend of mine was on his way to receive his degree, I launched my missile towards him. Unfortunately my aim was less than perfect and a venerable Hungarian mathematician, who had travelled far to collect an honorary Dublin doctorate, copped the lot. And as if on cue, the heavens opened, the rains fell, the flour became a dense white paste and I was forced to take sanctuary in the college chapel in order to escape the porters. But I didn't escape the day of judgement – I was expelled. The fun had finally ended.

Those days at Trinity have not been forgotten by Michael Chamberlayne either. Now a farmer and a director of the company that runs Headfort, following the sale of the estate, he remembers Jonah, twenty-five years ago,

wandering around the university in a duffle coat with a huge college scarf. He was a talented person in many ways. He was tremendously popular because he was such good company. He was always good for a laugh. He had a great sense of humour – never in the vindictive sense – and he was a great practical joker. Once, when we went into Commons for dinner, he dressed up a girlfriend of mine to look like a guy. Women were absolutely forbidden there, but here was this 'bloke' with a 36-inch bust beneath his Trinity gown coming into the dining room to eat with about 300 male students. I don't think the disguise was that successful but at least Jonah got her in.

Michael Chamberlayne, whose nickname 'Polly' had stuck with him since Headfort days, and Jonah would often spend part of their holidays together.

I remember one fine summer when I was staying with the Chamberlaynes, their water supply suddenly dried up and Polly and I were sent out on an 'oasis hunt' in his ancient green van. Polly was driving and I was crouched in the back, guarding an enormous empty beer barrel, the contents of which we had of course just been forced to put paid to in order to fill it with water. The journey was less than sedate and, as we rounded a sharp bend on two wheels, singing and shouting at the top of our voices, the barrel, with me in its path, careered into the rear door which immediately flew open. Somehow, the barrel managed to stay on board, but I was sent sailing backwards down the road. Polly, oblivious to my unscheduled departure, drove on for another half-mile or so before turning round to encourage me with the noisiest of choruses and found me gone. He turned the van around and hurtled back to where I was lying motionless on the verge. He thought I had killed myself, until I decided that he was worried enough and 'came back from beyond', cackling hysterically!

At Trinity, Barrington was by no means averse to the company of girls – an interest he had pursued with some success at Cheltenham – and the woman who loomed largest in his mind was Polly's sister, Pauline Chamberlayne, whom he had known since his prep school days at Headfort and then saw at Trinity when she came over from England to see her younger brother, his friends and her family. 'I always thought she was a smasher,' recalls Jonah. 'In simple terms, I was in love with her. She was a very zany creature then – very much the adored one.' Nevertheless, despite his ardour, it was not to be, and Pilly subsequently married Adrian Cowell, the documentary film-maker. Yet she still vividly remembers twisting all night with Jonah at a Trinity Ball he took her to. 'Jonah was lovely at Trinity. I wasn't surprised he became so successful, only that it happened so quickly. He just had something about him. I remember him saying to me that one day he would make a lot of money and be a success. He felt he was at a crossroads in his life in those days.'

Jonah's energies at Trinity were not always directed to his social life. Much of his time was devoted to sport. His talent for football showed itself in the university football team, on the rugby field he played for the 2nd XV, and he also played squash, though it was in his second year that he took up the game seriously and rapidly made the university team:

> It was suggested that as my brother was quite a good player, I should have some aptitude too. A game was arranged with the captain, John Gillam, just before the start of the 1960 season. Now I hadn't played for over a year but, for some extraordinary reason, I beat him. I imagine he must have been totally unfit and out of practice. I retained my No 2 position in the university team all that season during which we had two particularly enjoyable fixtures against the Guinness club, the Triflers. They were both away matches and afterwards there would be an eight-gallon barrel available for the six players and one or two shrewd supporters.

A report on the activities of the TCD squash club that season referred to one of those matches against the Triflers when Barrington played a certain G. Jackson: 'Although Barrington made full use of his wide variety of shots, Jackson constantly gained the centre of the court whenever Barrington attempted to beat him with a lob, for which Jackson, a current tennis international, was all too well equipped to deal. However, Barrington made every effort, particularly in the last stages of the game, when both players were very tired and made vital mistakes. His show of determination was rewarded with a 10–9 victory in the 5th game in a match in which for long periods he had been definitely outplayed.' Echoes of what was to come, perhaps?

Meanwhile, what had happened to Jonah's unofficial guardian? Under strict instructions from Major and Mrs

Barrington to look after their youngest son, Nikolai Tolstoy, by this time a well-groomed, distinguished-looking young man, some 6ft 4in tall, had other matters to occupy his mind. 'When Jonah arrived at Trinity, I was already in the swing of an established crowd. He quite rightly made his own friends, who were younger than I was, and so it was impossible to keep a close eye on him, even though Dublin is such a small city. I suppose I must accept a certain amount of blame for what happened to Jonah, but Trinity really was the wrong university for him. As far as he could see, no one appeared to be doing any work at all. He must have thought that everyone drank themselves silly and got into regular fights in bars. Perhaps I didn't set the best example because he would see me, ashen-faced, trotting into Trinity around midday, where we would all sit around drinking strong coffee before looking at our watches and saying "Right, when do the pubs open?" What he failed to realise was that the vast majority of us were hard at work when we weren't drinking and so managed to get our degrees. He could so easily have done the same as he was so very sharp-witted.'

Tolstoy and Barrington may not always have been in the same social set, but the Russian aristocrat clearly recalls one particularly rowdy evening which started as usual in a city pub:

We had just won a rather important rugby match and the atmosphere was even more highly charged than usual. Someone must have started a rumour that there were some rather charming nurses locked away in a nearby hostel, all eager to be rescued. So, after closing time, a number of us, including an especially enthusiastic Jonah, staggered around merrily until we found the place. We got through the walled gate and crept stealthily across the lawns and up to the windows. As we peered through, the curtains were suddenly flung wide and we found ourselves looking directly into the glowering sights of a large and draconian matron. With a speed that belied her bulk, she headed straight for the telephone, leaving us to seek refuge in a summer house in the garden where we regrouped ready for another attempt. Just as we thought the coast had cleared, the sound of approaching police cars caused us to alter our strategy and we decided to make a dash for it. It was a dark and cloudy night and, leading the charge, I went flying over a wheelbarrow and landed on my chin, cutting it rather badly. When we had all made it to the gate, we found our exit blocked by four rather large Kerry policemen. 'We were just walking in the garden in the cool of the night,' explained Jonah rather poetically. 'What's happened to your chin, then?' asked a Garda turning to me. 'Nothing at all,' I said, despite the fact that blood was now streaming from my face. 'Now listen to me,' said the sergeant, slamming shut his notebook. 'We all know it is the nurses themselves you've been after. But let me tell you one thing.' There was a worrying pause. 'You're all making the most terrible mistake to be sure. They're the ugliest lot you could wish to meet, so you'd better push off, and pretty quick, too.'

On one of his later visits to Marratons, Count Tolstoy was to receive a severe dressing-down from Mrs Barrington for abrogating his responsibilities to Jonah and his university career. Indeed her words were harsh enough to prompt Nikolai to storm out of the house and set off down the lane, until Jonah and the Major came running after him to set matters right – another example of a contretemps in the Barrington household that was soon forgotten.

For Barrington, his brief university career, although academically unsuccessful, was one of the happiest periods of his life, although, occasionally, the rather wayward path he was travelling along produced moments of self-doubt. 'Although the drinking bouts and riotous living were all very enjoyable, I was frustrated,' says Barrington. 'I was unable to get my teeth into anything. Throughout my time at Cheltenham and Trinity, I always thought I should be doing *something*, without really knowing what. I badly wanted to be successful in the sports area and I was constantly aware I was letting myself and my parents down dreadfully in the academic sense.'

Jonah returned home where, still brooding about his failures, he began to play football for the highly successful village football team. Just down the hill from Marratons was the field that served as the home of Morwenstow Football Club. It was here that the young men of Morwenstow could prove to the outside world that where they lived was more than just a collection of four small hamlets in the rugged terrain of North Cornwall:

> There was an astonishing competitive instinct in the village. The football club drew very large crowds to home games, and we would travel in convoys of coaches to watch away matches. One of my first sporting memories was of the village centre-forward, a man called Raymond Francis, who was always known as Turps after someone had seen him on a horse and thought he bore a resemblance to Dick Turpin. He was completely raw yet he had an enormous amount of natural talent. On one occasion, in a local derby match, Turps had been under constant fire from the crowd packed around the touchline. He decided that he had had enough, hit one of the spectators on the chin and broke his jaw. He was charged with assault and I can remember his friends coming round the parish to collect the money for his fine.

Turps still lives in Morwenstow, just down the road from Marratons and opposite the field where he scored so often for the village team. A small but tough-looking individual, he has never forgotten that touchline incident so many years ago: 'A spectator kept needling me and when he shouted out something I thought he shouldn't, I just went over and thumped him. I had to go to court at Camelford and was fined £47. I was suspended for four weeks and when I came back, I scored eight goals straight off. Then I was dropped because they didn't think I'd had a good game!'

Quite how anyone can be dropped from a football team after scoring eight goals in one match may be slightly difficult to comprehend. Maybe the village team was run by a Cornish Alf Ramsey who thought that work-rate was the most important quality in a footballer. Anyway, the time came when both Nick and Jonah played alongside Turps in that village football team during a period when it was enjoying unprecedented success. Nick, by now, was busy qualifying as a solicitor in Bude and, for the first time since their early childhood, the brothers found themselves together again, not in opposition, but in the same team. Invariably, Nick could be found in goal while Jonah was most often in the forward line at inside-left.

In April 1959, Morwenstow, captained by Nick Barrington, won the coveted Pickard Cup, beating Halwill before a large crowd at Pyworthy. Even by junior football standards, it was an extraordinary match judging by the headlines in the *North Devon Journal Herald* that read:

Five extra-time goals rob Halwill
of Pickard Cup
MORWENSTOW TRIUMPH

The *Herald*'s man at the match, Don Arnold, didn't leave too much doubt as to where his loyalties lay: 'So the Pickard Cup goes to Cornwall,' he wrote grudgingly. 'Morwenstow lifted the trophy at Pyworthy by winning 8–3 in extra time, but all my sympathies went to Halwill who fought magnificently and did enough in the first 90 minutes to deserve the cup.'

Five extra-time goals might seem to indicate a certain amount of superiority but Arnold clearly thought otherwise, pointing out that Halwill were playing their fourth game in five days. The score had been 3–3 after 90 minutes, Halwill having scored the equaliser in the last minute of full-time. But Morwenstow's five goals in extra time was 'the most fantastic goalburst seen in North Devon for many years', according to the *Western Times*, and Turps ended the game with four goals to his credit. 'There was enormous interest in the Pickard Cup,' says Jonah:

I passed the ball to Turps in extra-time and he went through the defence like an arrow from the halfway line, leaving four of them lying on the ground. He drilled the ball into the roof of the net from 20 yards out. It was a goal that would have been treasured at a Wembley Cup Final. In my mind's eye, I can still see Turps playing. He was brilliant. He'd score every week without fail. He had such natural talent – a powerhouse who could hit the ball with either foot. He was tremendously fast and elusive and very direct. If he gained possession he either scored, hit it wide or lost it to the opposition. He was uncontrollable. Goalkeepers were terrified of him because he would attack them after he had shot!

Nick was an especially good goalkeeper. He used to play in his glasses, and even though the fur would be flying all over the place – and there was a lot of indiscriminate kicking in these games – Nick would be in the middle of it all, diving at people's feet. We also had a terrific centre-half, Fred May, who was better than anyone else in the area. Then there was Turps of course and I reckoned I was pretty useful myself. I would get the ball in midfield, chip it across to Turps, and bang, end of story. I would never get the ball back from him.

That same winter Morwenstow completed the double, winning the Kingsley League with a 2–1 victory over Milton Damerel. In another 'unbiased' report, the *North Devon Journal Herald* recorded: 'According to the rules Milton Damerel should not have lost. They played far better soccer than their opponents although they fell short of perfection when it came to putting the ball into the net. It was not until the 20th minute that Morwenstow put their first goal into the Milton net. Inside-right Jonah Barrington broke away on the wing just inside the Morwenstow half. Beating two men on his dash towards the Milton goal, he crossed the ball to the waiting Francis, who sent it fair and square between the posts.' Unlucky Milton equalised with a penalty before, almost inevitably, Turps scored the winning goal in the 20th minute of the second half with a shot from outside the penalty area.

It was not until March 1962 that the 'unbeatables' were at last conquered when they lost a cup match 1–2 against Polruan. It was Morwenstow's first defeat for 15 months and ended a long run of 42 games without loss.

After his expulsion from Trinity, Barrington was to lead a nomadic existence for four years, driven by lack of money into a succession of jobs none of which held his attention for any great length of time. Ironically, in view of what later happened, he worked as an assistant groundsman at Bude Recreation Ground where his duties included sweeping out the squash court. He also worked as a local coalman for a coal merchant in Morwenstow, painted cottages in Devon for the poet Ronald Duncan, whose children were friends of the Barrington family, and had two teaching posts, one at a Yorkshire prep school and the other in the South of England.

During this period, too, he managed to acquire a criminal record during one of his visits to London to see Nikolai Tolstoy, who lived in a flat in Redcliffe Gardens in Earls Court just around the corner from Finch's, a famous London pub renowned for its draught Guinness.

'I was living with friends from Trinity and Jonah stayed with us on a sofa in my room,' recalls Tolstoy. 'Jonah had a devilish sense of humour. I can remember one night in Finch's we got so drunk we vaulted over the bar and began doling out free drinks to our friends. Faced with this mixture of muscle-power and cheerfulness, the bar staff did not seem interested in intervening. There was a woman there, a semi-hippy aged about 40, and Jonah and I in our drunken state chatted her up. Finally I reeled off to my flat and collapsed in bed. I remember waking up in the middle of the night with a splitting headache wondering where on earth I was when I heard this sepulchral voice, which I definitely recognised as Jonah's, coming from my sofa. "I have to leave you now, darling," said the voice. I thought it was a nightmare and fell asleep again.

'When I awoke in the morning and opened my eyes, there was this woman we had christened the Witch lying on my sofa. I said "What are you doing here?" "Oh," she said, "your friend Jonah said you are a frightfully kind gentleman who likes to put people like me up. He said I could stay here as long as I like." I was appalled. When I told her I had to get up, she said, "I don't mind", and got out her knitting. Downstairs I found Jonah and asked what was going on. Jonah burst out laughing. "You were very fond of the Witch last night," he said. "Last night is last night," I said, "and anyway she's your witch." Finally I managed to trick her out of the flat and she later told Jonah that his cruel friend had locked her out.'

One evening Barrington and Tolstoy graced a well-known Earls Court pub, The Scarsdale Arms, and matters got out of hand. Leaving the pub, the Tolstoy crowd came across some roadworks in the Earls Court Road. Tolstoy recalls how

one of our friends, Lawrence O'Shaughnessey, George Orwell's nephew, made an unsuccessful attempt to start a steamroller, Jonah jumped into a wheelbarrow and I started to wheel him off. At that time I was desperately in love with a girl I had been at university with. Having been close friends for several years without a proposal of marriage, she became engaged to a smooth Englishman called Bruce McPhail, who lived off the Fulham Road. Jonah, out of loyalty to a friend, immediately developed an intense dislike for this man whom he had never seen and he decided we should pay him a call and deposit the wheelbarrow on his doorstep. We were going down a mews when some kind woman told us the police were after us. Then we heard the sound of sirens. So we sprinted down a side street with a little Indian gentleman trotting beside us. Obviously he thought this was some strange English custom and felt we needed encouragement. Finally, as we emerged from the side street, two cars screeched to a halt and we were surrounded by the Chelsea Flying Squad.

Tolstoy and Barrington, still laughing and singing, were

taken to Chelsea police station, where the officers of the law viewed their claims of family background and lack of employment with grave suspicion. The following morning they appeared at West London Magistrates' Court to answer a charge of theft. The incongruity of waiting amongst an assortment of prostitutes for their case to come up left the two friends again in fits of laughter, and a police officer was prompted to tell them: 'This is a very serious case and I want you to remember that.' And so it proved. 'The Magistrate obviously thought we were a couple of layabouts and had decided from the outset that he was going to teach us a lesson,' recalls Jonah:

He conducted the case with utmost solemnity, which I found very funny in itself, and when our names were read out in full and I heard the clerk pronounce Nikolai Tolstoy-Miloslavsky and saw the magistrate's eyebrows shoot up, I began to shake with mirth. Luckily, at that stage, he either chose to ignore me or had failed to notice the state I was in, but when he turned to Nik and asked slowly and deliberately, 'Do you speak English?' I literally fell about. I mean, Nik had been educated at Wellington, one of the best-known English public schools. It was all too much for me and I remember this decent copper whispering urgently in my ear in an attempt to shut me up as I was definitely not helping my case. But worse was to come when an Irishman was wheeled in to view the wheelbarrow, which was then revealed as exhibit number one. He took the oath before being asked 'Seamus Ignatius O'Flaherty Donaghue, do you solemnly swear that this wheelbarrow is the property of the West London Tarmacadam and Asphalt Company?' I'm sure his sympathies were really with us because he took a long time to walk around the wheelbarrow before telling the court, 'Well, yer honour, it might be and there again it might not.' By this time the entire court was beginning to see the comedy and the magistrate, sensing that matters were getting out of hand, became very annoyed and quickly said, 'I think we'll take this as a positive identification.'

I think the whole case confused the poor man and he really didn't understand why we wanted to visit Bruce McPhail, let alone by wheelbarrow. He insisted that our defence, such as it was, was a 'tissue of lies' and finished off by describing our theft of the wheelbarrow as one of the most despicable cases of petty larceny it had ever been his misfortune to encounter and threatening us with prison. Then he hit us right below the belt and fined us £10 each. At once, my uncontrollable desire to laugh left me. Quite why we were convicted I still don't know. But in a strange way, I think this one incident brought me to my senses.

In retrospect, the saga of the wheelbarrow may have seemed like any one of the other pranks and escapades in which Jonah was involved. However, as he himself admits, it marked a crucial turning point. Before long, many of his friends would be remarking on an amazing transformation in his lifestyle. But the apparent contradiction was not illogical, for Jonah has never been one to take half measures and when he finally decided that his life was going to assume some direction and purpose, it certainly did.

In the summer of 1963, Jonah and Nikolai went on holiday to the South of France to the home of Nikolai's mother Mary, who lived with her second husband, the novelist Patrick O'Brian, in the beautiful village of Collioure. Nikolai well remembers Jonah's concern about the future at this time: 'Neither of us had proper jobs but at least I had come down from Trinity with a second in history. For his part, Jonah had tremendous physical energy and ambition but no sense of direction. He was also rather unhappy that none of his romantic entanglements had developed into a true relationship. One day he was quietly reading *Lorna Doone*. Suddenly he turned to me and said: "Do you think one day I'll find my Lorna Doone?" My mother and stepfather were terribly fond of Jonah and they told him that he could not go on doing nothing for ever.

Probably because he heard this advice from sympathetic outsiders, he listened.'

It seems that, after that holiday, Jonah did decide the time had come to find a worthwhile career, for in a letter to Mrs Barrington in December 1963, Tolstoy's mother wrote:

Thank you so much for your letter & the cheque & for the bank order which arrived this morning. You really should not have done it: you have all been so very kind to our Nikolai that it is we who are in your debt. We loved having Jonah & do hope he will come out again. It is sweet of you to say we influenced him but really it was he himself entirely: we merely agreed with him. I do think he is a dear & I am awfully glad he has taken hold of life because I am sure he will be so much happier. Please give him our fond love.

Before long, the young Cornishman who had been convicted of that 'despicable' crime in the Earls Court Road had found the direction for his life. It would provide a surprising contrast to the rakish existence he had led since arriving at Trinity College, Dublin.

5. The Monk of the West End

In the summer of 1964 Jonah Barrington received a telephone call at Marratons that was to end his years in the wilderness. John Mocatta, an Oxford graduate and a talented cricket and squash player, phoned to ask if Nick Barrington would like a game of squash. 'Mocatta was on holiday in Bude and mother answered the phone,' recalls Jonah. 'Nick was out but mother asked if I would give him a game. I hadn't played for three years, and I don't think I even had a racket. But I was so bored of sitting around that I went to Bude and played him. After he had given me a remorseless runaround, he asked what I was doing. I told him gloomily that I was totally unemployable but he didn't seem put off and said there was a clerical job going at the Squash Rackets Association in London and was I interested? You can imagine how I felt. I was willing to grasp at anything, certainly anything connected with sport. He went away and I heard nothing for about six weeks until, one morning, I received a letter from John Horry, the SRA secretary, asking if I was interested in the job. What a stroke of luck!'

So in September 1964, Jonah found himself working in London for the SRA as a clerical assistant. At that time squash was very much a minority sport, and the biggest court in the country was the Bruce Court at the Lansdowne Club in Berkeley Square where there were 144 seats and room for about 200 people to view a match from the gallery. Essentially squash was then a game for players rather than spectators, and its status was highlighted by that one tiny room in Regent Street from where John Horry ran the SRA single-handedly, with the help of an assistant only when funds permitted.

Horry was a formidable figure. Between the wars, he had

tried without success to become a Conservative MP, and had eventually settled for being party agent in the East End of London. His long association with the game of squash had begun in 1928 when, as an assistant district commissioner, he saw the Prince of Wales playing at the Muthaiga Club on the outskirts of Nairobi. Widely acknowledged as one of the game's most important administrators, he served the SRA as secretary from 1955 until his retirement in 1972, being awarded the MBE for his services to the sport. He made a point of employing assistants who wanted to improve their squash while helping him out with the more mundane administrative tasks at the SRA. Initially he was not over-impressed with Barrington: 'Jonah had hardly been touched by success . . . in fact he was in a pretty bad way because he had only just recovered from a back operation. I realised that he was rather desperate. His future was bleak and the fact that he could come to London, earn a bit of money and play squash was a godsend. He was more than an average squash player in those days but I saw nothing in his play to suggest he would ever become a world champion.'

Heaven-sent the opportunity may have been but it did not take Barrington long to become disillusioned with the job:

> The SRA headquarters was a particularly poky little room two flights up in an old building in Regent Street. If there were three people in the room, it was crowded. Basically I licked stamps, put addresses on envelopes, reeled off reams of duplicating material and answered the phone. And I was literally cooped up with this strange old gentleman, or at least he seemed old to me. He told me at some length that he had always had assistants who had been very useful squash players and that if they had been put together they could have beaten the England team. To make matters worse he told me that I was the worst assistant he had ever employed, either on the clerical or the playing side. The only one who could rival my administrative incompetence was Jonathan Smith,

51

said Horry, but at least he had been an England international.

John Horry was an amazing man, small, rotund, bespectacled, with a rather unusual voice. He had been in the colonial service and was a great character. Basically he *was* the SRA and spent a considerable amount of his own money entertaining on behalf of the association at his flat in Victoria. He worked all hours – even on Christmas Day. Later we moved to slightly more extensive premises in Park Crescent which we shared with the Central Council for Physical Recreation. I shared an office with a pleasant Canadian girl, who was a secretary with the Hockey Association, and I'll always remember the way Horry's head would appear around the door and he would say 'Just going to London.' Obviously we were in London but, to him, the City was London. When he returned, his head would appear again around the door and in his high-pitched voice he would ask: 'Anything to report?'

One day he went off to meet Charlie Waugh, the New Zealand champion, who was over to play in the British Amateur for the first time. When Horry returned, the door opened and he said: 'Anything to report?' I said 'No, but what's Charlie Waugh like?' 'Oh, very, very nice,' said John. 'Yes, really delightful, a charming fellow, but of course straight out of the trees.' I met Charlie later. He was indeed charming but he had very long arms, and actually he did look as if he was straight out of the trees! Horry was very amusing. Many years later, Major Ted Millman produced an excellent squash book with some rather odd drawings. The players in these drawings looked rather Eastern. When he reviewed the book for a magazine John Horry wrote that he thought it was very interesting, but from the illustrations it did seem that the Major was aiming at the Chinese market!

The Barrington who arrived in London in 1964 had represented his school, university, Bude Squash Club and his county Cornwall at the game without ever being ranked No 1 in any team. But he had never played the game seriously for any length of time. His nomadic existence following his abrupt departure from Trinity College, Dublin had had much to do with this. Jonah's relative lack of interest in the game at this stage could also be traced back to his great sporting rivalry with his brother. Because he had never been able to beat Nicholas at squash during their formative years, he had decided to concentrate on other sports such as tennis and football where his abilites were not in question. When Jonah went to work in London, there was no doubt which of the brothers was the better squash player, for Nick was already the Cornish champion.

Jonah's initial attempts to develop his squash in London met with little success. No doubt Mocatta, a member of Hampstead, thought there might be a place for Jonah in his club's Cumberland Cup side if he got that job with the SRA. But, sadly, the club team proved too strong for Jonah to win a permanent place in it:

When Mocatta saw that I was not going to live up to his early expectations, his interest in me waned. John Horry was also disappointed in my progress. What condemned me most in his eyes was a match I played with Ken Williamson of Durham. He was a very useful performer but not really up to the London standard. He made every mistake in the book but he was still fiercely competitive. Potentially I was much the better player but he didn't allow me to play – he was a master gamesman, one of the finest amateur sportsmen of the day. We played at the Seymour Hall Baths and he beat me in five. In Horry's eyes, this condemned me to total anonymity.

During those first couple of months in London, I was still terribly depressed. Although I was beginning to feel that my rhythm was improving and my movement becoming more natural. I didn't seem to be making any progress. I wasn't beating anybody. Eventually I decided I had had enough, so I went to

Horry and told him that I would be better off in Bude, as nobody would play me in London. But Horry listened carefully and assured me he would do something about the situation. He was as good as his word and approached Nasrullah Khan, the Pakistani coach, to see if he would help me. But Nasrullah had only recently moved to the Lansdowne Club where he was only allowed to coach members. Undaunted, Horry tried another tack. As chairman of the Escorts Club he took me up to Norfolk to play for them. I didn't think he was impressed, though. I suppose I seemed to him to be no more than an honest journeyman.

But Barrington's game was soon to improve dramatically. Abandoning his glasses, he decided to play in contact lenses.

I found them absolutely marvellous. No more steamed-up glasses on hot courts. I can't think how I ever managed without them. Everybody laughs when I haven't got my lenses in because I really am very short-sighted. At the West Warwicks Squash Club in Birmingham, I sometimes run without them and afterwards in the shower, people must think I'm being rude because I don't talk to them. But the real reason is that I can't even see them! The optician once told me that I might be short-sighted but I have good eyes. When the adjustment was made, my sight would be very good. How I can have good eyesight when I can't see I've never been able to understand.

I first used the contact lenses in the summer of 1964 but it was three months before I could get accustomed to putting them in. At first it seemed like having gravel permanently in my eyes. One Saturday, after playing football in them for Kenton Town in the Middlesex League, I had to dash down to South London to play a squash match for a Major Millman 'Select' against the Dulwich Club. I had left my lenses in to save time but, on arrival at the club, I found I had mislaid my spectacles – so it was the lenses or nothing. My first-ever match with the contacts was against Jack Dengel and, after a bit of a battle, I holed out in five. I remember being thrilled because, in spite of the odd hiccup, the lenses were fantastic. Suddenly, at the age of 23, I could see!

In 1967, when I was in New Zealand, I went to a specialist because I began having a lot of trouble again with my eyes. He made me take the lenses out and put them in again. When he saw me licking them, which was a favourite ploy, he really ripped into me. He gave me a lecture on infections and told me I was lucky I wasn't blind. He taught me how to put them in and take them out properly and said it was ridiculous I didn't wear them all day. I still have those original lenses – the hard type – and I've become so accustomed to them that unless I'm talking about them, I wouldn't even know I've got them in.

Apart from the miracle of the contact lenses, there was another very good reason why Barrington's latent talent began to surface in such a spectacular fashion. He was playing with increasing regularity and he had also become a fitness fanatic.

The future England international Paul Millman joined Jonah in his quest for stardom. The son of Major Ted Millman, the professional who had coached Barrington in his schooldays, Paul had also been a pupil at Cheltenham College, but not until after Jonah had left. He, too, had come to London in 1964 determined to improve his squash, and had got a job at Lillywhites, the well-known Piccadilly store. A fine strokeplayer, Millman is remembered for a remark he made after winning the plate event in the inaugural world championships: 'I must be the world's best worst player'. Now a marketing executive with Harp Lager and chairman of the SRA's executive committee, Millman still remembers his first meeting with Jonah in London:

I was trying to flog squash rackets in our sports department when Jonah turned up. He wore glasses then and it wouldn't be too unkind to say that he was a fairly insignificant-looking individual. Nevertheless we got talking and as we had both come to London for the same reason, we just started training and playing together. I had a bedsitter in West Hampstead near Hampstead Squash Club so we would play there and train on the cricket field even though we didn't really know what we were doing. Every night we either trained or took part in matches, in addition to the odd SRA match fixed up by John Horry and a few tournaments. At that stage, I was more successful than Jonah. I beat him 3–0 in the Middlesex Championships. Unlike him, I had been the school No 1 with a good record in junior tournaments. He was basically a retriever and, like many left-handers, had a weakness on the backhand. He just hacked the ball and ran around the court; there was no science to his game. But he was fitter than I was, he trained harder than I did and he could certainly outrun me. At that time, internationals like Michael Oddy and Richard Boddington played a lot and worked very hard at their game. But they were not taking the all-consuming route that Jonah was. We would play a game at Hampstead and then go squelching around the cricket field in the dark. People thought we were out of our minds and they stood around the bar saying we hadn't got a chance – particularly Jonah, because they fervently believed he was a no-hoper. And indeed the evidence suggested they were right.

But no one realised just how seriously Jonah was prepared to take the game. He took it by the scruff of the neck in a very single-minded way. He began running miles and miles while, on court in practice, he would hit the ball relentlessly up and down the wall.

The classic route to the top in British squash at the time was to get a Blue at Oxford or Cambridge. Jonah's methods were regarded as naive and slightly peculiar. I would go running with him but, after a while, would tail off. I just couldn't keep it up. If he went on a ten-mile run, I always had to peel off after five miles. He would run 25 or 30 times around the cricket field, or if not at Hampstead Cricket Club, then in Green Park. He wasn't really a born athlete but he certainly made himself into one. He became a very good runner.

His enthusiasm rubbed off on me. We had a mutual sense of ambition but I could never hope to match his dedication. He is the most single-minded sportsman I have ever met; his training schedules were incredible. Working at the SRA, he would have a game at the White House at lunchtime and then a long run after work. Alternatively we would lift weights at the old Mayfair Gym in Paddington Street, Marylebone, for two hours, before getting a bus down to the Lansdowne where we would always have a court for the last hour from 8 to 9pm. We were often so tired from lifting all those weights that we could hardly hit the ball and we had some pretty dreadful games. We would then do endless press-ups before relaxing by the swimming pool, eating, and then going home absolutely shattered. This would be the pattern for the whole week. Jonah could always cope with a far greater amount of physical work than I could. He would go for a run in the mornings before work as well. We would also spend the weekends almost entirely at the Lansdowne, we would play in the morning, relax in front of the television for an hour or so after lunch, play again in the afternoon and then go to a film or watch television in the evening.

In the summer of 1965, Paul Millman returned to Gloucestershire to play cricket hoping to find a regular place in the county side. 'When I came back to London and played Jonah, there was a hell of a difference,' Paul recalls. 'He had played all through that summer against better players and he had substantially improved his racket skills and was tremendously fit. Now it was I who was being seen off pretty rapidly. From just rushing around getting the ball back, he was now retrieving it with skill and placing it just where he wanted. He had also developed a straight drop shot. The talent was beginning to show through. He *looked* like a squash player and, because he had improved so much, he took many opponents by surprise. He had come from nowhere and no one knew what to expect.'

While Paul Millman found Barrington's enthusiasm infectious, other older, established players were not so impressed. When Mike Corby first came across the young man from Cornwall, he regarded him with total disdain, for Corby was a games player in the Corinthian mould, a sporting cavalier with so much natural talent that he was able to remain at the top for a considerable time, living the life of a playboy sportsman. He first played squash for England in 1963, a year before Jonah's arrival in London, eventually representing Great Britain and England 37 times, and playing international hockey, too, on 92 occasions. Lethal with the ladies, Corby was not a man to be restricted by convention and he once displayed his independent and mischievous spirit by returning to the RAC Club, from which he had been banned for breaking the club's dress regulations, wearing a white silk tie – on court! Many people felt Corby wasted his great talents. But if he had been totally dedicated, he would not have been Mike Corby.

Corby's first impression of Barrington, at the Lansdowne Club, was in no way complimentary:

He was basically a drip. He was skinny, he had a shortish dark hairstyle, he wore horn-rimmed glasses, there wasn't a muscle on him and he had a terrible style on court. I came to see him as just a pleasant bloke who talked in an amusing fashion about, for instance, how he had been an alcoholic. He would always watch me playing, and that's how I got to know him better. I was recognized as a reasonable amateur sportsman and one day the inevitable happened and he asked if he could have a hit with me. Frankly I avoided it. I tried to make sure I was not in a position to play him – one always wanted to play someone of one's own standard or better.

Despite this unpromising beginning, Barrington and Corby were to become good friends, for, although on court they were a complete contrast, off court they were both highly articulate sportsmen with good senses of humour and a similar streak of rebellion in their make-up. It was not long, therefore, before Corby agreed to play Jonah:

I was very easy on him because, frankly, he was not very good. I knew in my heart of hearts he had absolutely no chance of achieving what he said he was going to do, namely win the World Championship. It was a laughable suggestion. But we played all the same and, surprisingly enough, we got on quite well. After every match he used to put his towel down and do his sit-ups, press-ups and stomach-curls waving his legs in the air. It was bloody funny to watch at first, and then you started respecting him, liking him the more for it. We all trained, it was a question of degree. At that time, squash was a gentleman's game and people pretended they didn't train. But suddenly here was a bloke, who was not a professional, physically training hard in front of everyone else.

Before long, Corby was to find that the player with absolutely no chance had developed dramatically. 'I remember one summer he worked hard and improved substantially. By then he was the Cornish county champion and he had become a real handful on court – all based on his theory of fitness. Finally it became clear that Jonah had something more than I did. It certainly wasn't talent – I always had more of that than he did. But he had phenomenal determination. He didn't have speed but he did put pressure on you. His was a disciplined mind: he would play down the wall, down the wall, then play one drop, then down the wall, down the wall and then play another drop shot. He used to say to me, '"Tricky", 45 minutes the first game'. I won the first game in my first Amateur final against him in 38 minutes. But he'd drawn out the sting. He'd wear you down. A great tactician.'

While those around him looked upon Barrington as

something of an oddity, Jonah was becoming super-fit and learning the game all the time. Each defeat provided another lesson, every hour spent endlessly hitting that ball up and down the court in lonely practice sessions was improving his ball control. As he discovered a fault, he would correct it:

> I remember playing a South African, John Roy, who was in the Hampstead team. He boasted the ball a lot and I just couldn't do anything at all about it. After a couple of games, he explained the reason. I was a front wall starer. When the ball was hit behind me, I never turned to look. I just waited for the ball to reappear on the front wall again. He taught me the fundamental lesson of turning round to see your opponent making his shot and gaining the extra time to play your own shot. When I originally went to Hampstead, they all beat me. I had one or two matches for the team when they were short of players. Then I played in the club championship and beat them all. In the summers of 1965 and 1966, I was devoting my whole life to squash and I improved more than at any time during my career. I seemed to get better every day. During the summer, you were meant to have a rest from the game otherwise you would get stale. It was not the done thing to play all the time. When I worked at Bude Recreation Ground, they had table tennis tables on the squash court in the summer months because no one would ever dream of playing squash then. But while other people were having a rest from the game, I had four squash seasons in two years.

After five months in London, Barrington's progress was reflected in some impressive results, one of which was the achievement of a significant personal landmark when he beat his brother Nicholas for the first time in the Bude Invitation Tournament in January 1965. The score in the final was 9–1, 9–7, 9–1 and for Jonah this victory constituted a very real psychological breakthrough for he had always had tremendous respect for his brother's sporting ability: 'Physically Nick was a very strong boy. He was 6ft 4in tall, beautifully built, very quick with a long stride and a far better natural runner than I was. If Nick had had the same desire as me to succeed in sport, I am sure he would have been absolutely exceptional, possibly as an athlete. But he never really developed his potential to the full. At Cheltenham College, he was one of the best junior squash players in the country. When I went to London, Nick was the Cornish No 1 and I was determined one day to beat him. When I did, I was absolutely thrilled.' Nick remembers that defeat, too, for he was never to beat his brother again: 'I was not too happy. A lot of strings had gone on my racket and there was a dispute about whether I could borrow another. But it was obvious Jonah had improved. He just did everything so much better.'

Later that same season, on his way to winning the Cornish championship Jonah again beat his brother and, by this time, he was beginning to find his way on the competitive circuit. In January 1965, having won two matches in the eliminating competition, Barrington took part in the British Amateur for the first time beating the Australian, Jim Moore, in the first round, 9–5, 9–4, 0–9, 9–6, before losing to Sherif Afifi 7–9, 7–9, 2–9 in the second round. 'I tried very hard against Sherif but he made me twist and turn so many times that my knees were still wobbly three days later. But I will always remember that he was extremely good to me. At the time he was very much better than me, but, with his compatriot Samir Nadim, he was one of the few players who would always give me a game. In practice games he was always most helpful and in that championship match I suspect he also gave me a few points here and there.'

In the East of England Championships in February, Jonah won three matches, including a victory over Ken Davidson, a previous winner, before losing to John Ward 4–9, 6–9, 9–3, 2–9. Each time he played Ward, however, he seemed to come up against a major psychological stumbling block. In the Inter-County Plate Competition in March, he was again decisively beaten by Ward 1–9, 4–9, 1–9, as

Hampshire defeated Cornwall 5–0 at Bournemouth. 'Ward absolutely destroyed me,' recalls Barrington. 'He was the rising star that season and getting very close to England standard. I was so frustrated afterwards that the tears flowed down my face. Here I was making all this effort and each time I played Ward I seemed to do worse.'

In April, Barrington reached the final of the West of England Championships losing two games to three to Sharif Khan after beating Nigel Faulks, who was graded above him. He was in fact detailed by John Horry to run that tournament – a change from licking stamps – and this gave him the chance to meet the remarkable Jonathan Smith:

Jon had entered the tournament while he was in the South of France and on Friday night, when there was still no sign of him, his opponent was getting rather fed up. While I was trying to placate him, a telegram appeared from Smith saying 'Am arriving fast'. About four o'clock in the morning, Jon called from a telephone box saying he had landed at Dover and was heading westwards. He couldn't make the morning match so we delayed the start until the afternoon. Jon arrived and beat his opponent, who was a pretty good player, without any trouble at all. He was very small, well-built and very absent-minded, although he had no difficulty in quoting verbatim much of the works of Shakespeare. When he appeared wearing one brown and one red sock, he always used to say: 'I've got another pair like this at home'. We became friends and, later, one day after I had played him at the Lansdowne, I had another match immediately afterwards and I couldn't find my second set of kit. I soon found that my lovely clean gear had been running around the court with me – on Jonathan Smith! He frequently used to arrive without kit and plunder someone's locker.

Jonathan was a great character and he saved me financially on more than one occasion. I was very lucky to know such an extraordinary individual. He lived in Brighton in a block of flats with communal bathrooms. One night, or to be more accurate near dawn, he was overtaken by the call of nature and, naked as was his custom, he slipped out of his room, nipped into the bathroom, and then headed back to bed. Unfortunately, in his absence, his door had closed firmly to. He was in a right old fix. He returned to the chilly bathroom to review his predicament. Suddenly he recalled that there were some old squash clothes in his car. The drawback was that the car was parked some 600 yards down the Brighton front. Undeterred as always, only one decision was possible. So it was that a Brighton milkman and some early morning risers were startled to see my brave young friend doing an Olympic streak along the front as a rather chilly dawn broke over the sea!

After spending the summer of 1965 training at Hampstead Cricket Club, Barrington won the South of England Championships in October beating Sharif Khan for the first time 9–1, 9–6, 0–9, 9–7 in the semi-final and then at last defeating the dreaded John Ward 9–7, 9–0, 10–8 in the final. Later a victory over Mike Corby earned him a reserve place in the British team against Australia and, playing No 4, he defeated Cam Nancarrow. It was a somewhat lucky win, but nevertheless it was a victory over a world-class player on a big occasion. In the British Amateur in January 1966, Barrington was destroyed by the England international Richard Boddington 1–9, 7–9, 2–9 and the defeat brought on a deep depression. In February, Barrington played for Ireland for the first time losing 3–9, 10–8, 9–4, 5–9, 3–9 to the England No 1 Jeremy Lyon as his country were beaten 5–0 at the RAC Club. 'I asked my father whether he would prefer me to play for Ireland or England,' says Jonah. 'That is what determined my choice and not the fact that I had the chance to be the Irish No 1 instead of the England No 4. That was of no consequence as I had no intention of remaining anyone's No 4 for very long.' Another factor in the decision was that Barrington had accumulated debts amounting to around £200, a considerable sum in those days, and two members of the Irish team, Barton Kilcoyne and Donald Pratt, bailed him out with some much-needed money.

When Ireland played Scotland, Barrington was beaten in straight games by Ollie Balfour and it was not until Ireland played Wales that he had his first win in Irish colours, beating the Welsh No 1 Peter Stokes 3–1. In the winter of 1965–6, Barrington won three other titles – defeating Sharif Khan in the final of both the North of England Championships and the West of England Championships, and beating Tony Gathercole 3–0 to win the Isle of Wight Championship. The man who never stopped training was now no longer a player who could be ignored.

However, during the long period in which Barrington was struggling to establish himself as a leading British player, he never lost faith with himself. But, he affirms, he could not have fought the fight without the man who inspired him to remain on the battlefield – the great Pakistani coach, Nasrullah Khan. One day in 1962, Jonah was at the Junior Carlton Club watching a couple of friends from the gallery.

As I watched, I remember thinking quite clearly that I was a damn sight better than both of them put together and that perhaps I really ought to make a concerted effort to improve. Suddenly, my thoughts were disturbed as the gallery door opened and a stocky, balding Pakistani came in. He had piercing eyes and a very powerful face; as a young man he must have had the proud look of an eagle. This was Nasrullah Khan, resident professional at the Junior Carlton, a member of the great Khan family, and the man who had guided his brother Roshan to victory against Hashim in the 1957 British Open. There was no doubt that there was an aura about the man. I was instinctively aware that he knew more about the game of squash than anyone I had ever met.

I plucked up courage and went over to speak to him. I told him I was going back to Cornwall, that I desperately wanted to become a better squash player, but that I lived eight miles away from the nearest squash court, in Bude. He listened to me with great patience, then replied quietly: 'You must bicycle to the squash court or, if you can, run; it is very good thing. And when you get to the court, you must practise. You must hit the ball up one side wall one hundred times. This very good thing. Then you hit the ball up other side wall one hundred times. This very good thing. And you must skip on court. This very good thing, very good practice. This will make you very good squash player.'

That advice from the small Pakistani with the patrician air may have had an almost comic simplicity coming from a man obviously not entirely at home with the English language. But Nasrullah Khan was regarded as the finest teacher of the game in England and he provided Barrington with advice about two fundamentals of the game of squash – fitness and ball control. Very few players have the patience to hit a squash ball up and down the court a hundred times on both their forehand and backhand. But Nasrullah's advice was not lost on Barrington: 'Instinct told me that if I was ever going to learn then this was the man to teach me. Never for one moment did I doubt him.'

Nasrullah was an exceptional sportsman. 'When Naz arrived in England for the first time, he had to take tennis and squash tests before he could be accepted as a coach. I think it was Bill Moss, the British professional tennis champion, who was delegated to give Naz the tennis test. I know how shocked Moss was when Naz beat him 6–3, 6–2. He was in fact a lovely tennis player. I can remember a crowd of us getting together to play tennis one day and Naz, who was about 48 at the time, had not picked up a tennis racket for three or four years. But the moment he started to play, we immediately saw his beautiful technique. It was as if he had never played squash in his life.'

This then was the man who was to guide Barrington to the world championship. But during his first year in London, Jonah was unable to become directly involved with Nasrullah as by then the Pakistani was the coach at the Lansdowne Club and the membership fee was something Barrington simply could not afford. But although Nasrullah was not allowed to coach Barrington, his influence was certainly there. Jonah made sure that he saw him regularly, either through his job at the Squash Rackets Association or at the Lansdowne when he played as Paul Millman's guest: 'While I was going through these strenuous training routines in the summer of 1965, I was still not being coached directly by Nasrullah, even though I seemed to spend more time at the Lansdowne than most of their members. Perhaps I wasn't allowed to have any lessons from him but I preyed on him incessantly. If he sat down, I sat down immediately next to him and started talking. He was an exceptionally nice, courteous person and he couldn't get away from me. I was always asking him what I should do.'

That Barrington could be so dedicated was even more remarkable considering his daily confrontation with the obvious distractions of 'Swinging London'.. While his contemporaries were forever going to parties or promenading up and down the Kings Road, Jonah was not to be found in the pubs and clubs where he had formerly blazed a drunken trail. 'I had a fetish about not taking liquid at the time. For about two years, I scarcely had even a glass of water. I never touched orange squash but if I was really thirsty, I drank milk or orange juice. People must have thought me very odd but I didn't feel I was missing out on anything; in any event, my salary was only about £600 a year and I was constantly in debt, so I didn't really mind. I was totally consumed with a fever to become the best squash player in the world. Indeed, after my first four months in London, I decided that this was to be my sole objective. It was not just my primary purpose; it was the be-all and end-all of my existence. I wasn't going to allow anything to distract me. I trained day after day, week after week, month after month. I exercised with intensity – I didn't have a recovery period. I was unashamedly fanatical, intolerant of others who did not show the same dedication, and failed to realise that what is best for one person might not be right for someone else. Mike Corby, for example, was a very imaginative squash player, he was always fresh on court, but if he applied himself as I did he might well have dulled his spirit.'

Jonah's running programme, which took him through the streets of London, attracted a good deal of ridicule, for those were the days before running and jogging had become a national pastime:

> During the summer, I would get up at about seven in the morning and put on longjohns, a big woolly tracksuit and white plimsolls. People would shout ribald remarks as I went by, but I didn't really hear them. I must have been quite a sight and local cats, taking a leisurely walk home after their night on the tiles, would take one look at me bearing down on them and flee for the nearest refuge, howling madly!
>
> My running territory included Brompton Cemetery where I used to stop for a chat with the people working there. We seemed to get on really well and I found out later that they were outside-duty prisoners from Wormwood Scrubs. Perhaps there's a lesson to be learned there!
>
> After my run, I would have a cup of coffee before going off to work at the SRA. In the middle of the day, I would play squash at the White House, which was an expensive business because it was two shillings in the meter for ten minutes on court. In the evening, I would catch the tube from Regent's Park to West Hampstead where, after buying a pint of milk, I always made my way to Hampstead Cricket Club to spend two hours on court practising all kinds of shots, skipping and doing exercises. I loved the Hampstead club; they were a very friendly crowd. But I suppose I must have seemed rather anti-social. Like my father, I loved talking to people but I rarely went near the bar because I couldn't afford to buy anyone else a drink.

Later when Barrington had found success, his extraordinary lifestyle was to capture the imagination of the national newspapers. Here was an amateur sportsman devoting his life to a game in the days when dedication was seen as fanaticism. It was true that amateur athletes embarked on exacting training schedules and made tremendous sacrifices in order to succeed at international level. But athletes generally fitted in their training schedules between work. With Barrington it was rather different. Squash was going to be his career even if it offered no great financial rewards and, working for the SRA, he was not merely encouraged to play squash, it was expected of him. Traditionally the SRA post allowed for the fact that Horry's assistant was unlikely to be embarking on a full-time clerical career, but even though Jonah was accorded every opportunity to develop his talents as a player, he decided after a while that even the liberal existence he enjoyed under Horry did not give him enough time for the task in hand: 'After about a year at the SRA, I realised I was going to need more and more time to do what I needed to do. Then, one morning in December 1965, Horry rang me up at 7.15 and told me to be in the office by 8.45. I was never very punctual. "Hang on," I said, "I'm playing Tewfik Shafik in the quarter final of the British Open tonight", and at once Horry put the phone down. I was very angry. After all, this was the most important squash match I had ever played. That evening I lost to Shafik after having led him in every single game. He was more experienced, true, but after the defeat, I decided to pack in the SRA job.'

While Horry usually took a lenient view of Jonah's lack of punctuality and general incompetence, on that particular day he really did need his assistant's help: 'That day we had to get out the draw for the British Amateur Championship, which meant putting four or five papers in each envelope and sending them off. I don't think Jonah took too kindly to the rather menial tasks I gave him and when I asked him to come in early, he blew up. It was only for one day but that evening he was going to play a match in the Open. We had words and I told him that if he didn't want to do the work, I'd get somebody else, and that was that.'

There was a final postscript to the SRA job. 'What happened was that I hadn't kept up my insurance stamp money,' recalls Jonah. 'John gave me something like £43 to get the stamps for my card. I hadn't any money at all and suddenly I had been given £43. This would be rather useful,

I thought. And it was. Of course, after some weeks, it came to his notice what had happened. After I had left the SRA, I would get these messages about the stamp money, asking when I was going to repay him. Finally John wrote me a classic letter. It simply stated: "Dear Jonah, I would like to remind you that as far as we know there are no facilities for Squash Rackets in Her Majesty's prisons."'

Barrington was rather fortunate to be living with sympathetic flatmates:

After leaving the SRA I had a succession of part-time jobs. For a term I found myself teaching, amongst others, Japanese children French and Divinity at a school in Queensgate, and I had a milk round in the Earls Court area that involved getting up at the ridiculously early hour of 4.45 am. Sometimes when I finished my round at about 11 am, I just felt like going to bed for about ten hours, but of course I had to start training. So I would make do with just an hour's nap. I also took a job posing for art students as a nude model – it was a rather daunting experience sitting in the buff in front of a load of students, I can tell you, but without my glasses I couldn't see a thing, so I felt rather like the proverbial ostrich. Later during the summer, I underwent the appalling experience of being a dishwasher in a South Kensington bistro. My hours were from 6.30 pm until 1.00 am and I have good reason to recall that it was a particularly warm August and September. Greasy plates, cups, saucers, glasses, cutlery and saucepans seemed to arrive in ever-increasing quantities. The water got filthier, the kitchen grew noisier, the place got hotter and eventually my mind ceased to function and a sort of robotic reflex took over. Dante's Inferno will always seem like the Chapel of Rest after that.

The life of a milkman, nude model and dishwasher hardly left me with energy for training but I refused to relax my schedules until, very early one morning, I was climbing the stairs back to the flat thinking what a great contribution the inventor of rubber gloves had made to society when I literally began to fade out like a dying ember. The next thing I remember is waking up in the flat and being lectured to in no uncertain terms by one of my flatmates, a Canadian called David Elliot, who was a geology research student at London University. He told me categorically that I was never to look at a pile of dirty plates again and that, if necessary, he would finance me for the rest of my squash career rather than see me in this sort of state.

David and all the other people in the flat, Chris Kendall, Robin Waddell, Wally Johnson and Geoff Lemon, were all great supporters. They lived the journey with me, helped me fight my battles and paid for my recovery. I will always be grateful to them.

For Barrington, survival was to mean relying increasingly on the financial help of other people. Mike Corby remembers how good Barrington was at surviving on rather limited funds. 'In some ways it was wonderful to watch Jonah playing the pauper. It developed into a real art form. He never had any money. It was always "Have you got a ball?" "Can I borrow your racket?" "Have you got two bob on you for a sandwich?"'

As Barrington began to show that he might indeed reach the top as a squash player, the support increased. Barton Kilcoyne and Donald Pratt, the leading Irish players when Jonah had been at Trinity, were anxious that Jonah should play for Ireland and they proved good friends:

I was practising at Hampstead one day when Barton Kilcoyne appeared in the gallery. I had played him in handicap tournaments when I was a student but had never beaten him. Out of the blue, he asked me if I would be interested in playing for Ireland and, of course, I jumped at the chance. Later, both Barton and Donald Pratt offered to finance me through 1966 and into 1967 and I was only too relieved to take them up. Nothing appealed to me more than the prospect of an end to the interminable part-time jobs and the

70

thought that I would not have to go back into an office. The money was paid into my bank account on a monthly basis – I can't recall how much it was – but it was sufficient for me to become a full-time operator because my overheads were minimal. In the terminology of the day, I was a shamateur and I suppose that if the details had leaked out, I would have lost my amateur status. But there have always seemed to be double standards and when the Scottish player Mike Oddy was preparing for the Open, I argued forcibly that he was in effect a full-time player, for his father was very wealthy and he had never had to work for any sustained period. In my case, my argument was simple: for father read Kilcoyne and Pratt. I must say that I liked that Irish connection; Barton and Donald were such good-humoured people. Life for them was fun and there was always laughter when they were around. What a contrast to the English scene which was full of upper-crust stuffiness.

The single-mindedness of Barrington's attitude to squash was beginning to provide a talking point throughout sporting circles and, before long, the press recognised the novelty of his approach. Various reports referred to him as 'The Monk of the West End' and even 'The Fittest Man in the World'. Such phrases were not without their basis in fact, for what he was doing was, at that time, so untypical of a British sportsman and, in the world of squash, quite unheard of. After all, this was not a sport that called for strenuous training routines and no one played the game throughout the year lest they risk the awful penalty of becoming stale.

But as Jonah's first two years in London slipped by, the key question remained unanswered. Was there the remotest chance that what Corby had described as 'Barrington's brilliant gamble' could pay off?

6. Champion of the World

When Barrington first met Nasrullah Khan in 1962, he instinctively sensed that this was the man who would transform him into a formidable squash player. For was this not an important member of a remarkable Pakistani sporting dynasty that had dominated world squash and produced four world champions, who between them had won thirteen consecutive British Open titles between 1951 and 1962? Remarkably, Hashim, Azam, Roshan and Mohibullah all came from the village of Nawakilla a mile from the North-West Frontier city of Peshawar. They were all Pathans, the proud warrior race which the British Army had never been able to conquer, and they were all members of the same tribe that had settled in the plains rather than the hills.

It was Hashim who became the most famous of the Khans. The son of the chief steward at the Peshawar Club, he learned to play squash on the two roofless courts built for the pleasure of the British in 1901. He had come to Britain in his mid-thirties and won the British Open a record seven times (1951–6 inclusive and 1958) before departing to North America to seek further fame and fortune. Well known for his remarkable speed, the barrel-chested Hashim was regarded by many as the game's greatest player. 'The rubber shrieked on the floor as Hashim turned,' said the British player Brian Phillips. 'He could be wrong-footed but it didn't make any difference.'

Hashim's younger brother Azam was also in the same class. Nine years younger, he lost to Hashim in three Open finals but later won four consecutive Open finals (1959–61) before an achilles tendon injury ended his competitive career. In Rex Bellamy's book, *The Story of Squash,* the Scottish player Michael Oddy regards Azam as the greatest:

'He was the perfect orthodox player . . . everything was absolutely right. He could play a drop-volley from anywhere, from anything the slightest bit loose. His accuracy of shot was quite phenomenal. He was a raw beginner when he started playing under Hashim . . . but I think he could have won the last two of Hashim's Opens (towards the end he was carrying his brother).'

Then there was Roshan, cousin of Hashim and Azam and brother of Nasrullah, who, although he only ever won one Open title, in 1957, was regarded as the best strokeplayer of the trio. Finally there was Mohibullah, son of Hashim's sister, who, although not in quite the same league as the others, also won one Open. His spectacular acrobatic qualities had once reduced a female spectator at the Lansdowne Club to a state of terror as his momentum took him up the back wall in a vain attempt to retrieve the ball.

The Khans were numbered by many among the gods of squash. Dick Hawkey, one English player frequently faced with the task of confronting the Pakistani masters, has never had the slightest hesitation in declaring that Hashim, Azam and Roshan were streets ahead of any other talent there was, or ever will be. And to think that many other talented Pakistani players were never given an opportunity to come to England. Squash history would indeed have made very different reading if they had been.

There are many tales surrounding the brilliance of the Pakistanis but Barrington recalls with amusement one particular incident in which the Welshman Denis Hughes, one of the great strokemakers in the history of the sport, encountered such a player.

Denis was out in Pakistan during the early 1960s and was having a thoroughly enjoyable and successful time until he was approached one day by a venerable gentleman, well into his seventies, sporting a long white beard. Well, Denis couldn't really believe it when the old man politely asked for a game. Nevertheless, he agreed, but his challenger courteously insisted that the game should commence at seven in the morning. This rather horrified Denis as he had never been out of bed at such an ungodly hour in his life, but there he was the following morning, albeit slightly amused, ready to play. The sun was up and already you could have fried an egg on the floor of the roofless concrete court, that is if you didn't mind the liberal quantities of dust. Now, in dusty conditions you almost have to be an Olympic skater because if you can't slide around, the odds are set against you and no mistake. 'Mr Hughes', inquired the sage deferentially, 'would you care to play the best of 9 or 11 games?' Poor old Denis couldn't believe it: I'm sure he still thought he was safely tucked up in bed. However, the moment play began, he was left in no doubt whatsoever that this was for real. The old man ran him off the court.

Nasrullah Khan was part of this squash dynasty and now, at long last, the young Cornishman finally achieved his aim and became his pupil. However, until Jonah could join the Lansdowne Club there could be no formal link between them. Thus, in the autumn of 1965, Jonah's brother Nick and Nasrullah decided that something would have to be done and so, with themselves as main benefactors, they organised a collection to raise the membership fee of £30, a sum which had for so long daunted Jonah. It is difficult to contemplate what would have happened to Barrington's career, or indeed his life, had they not achieved their target.

No sooner had Jonah become a member of the Lansdowne than he was eager to begin the hard work in earnest. But first the master had to assess his new pupil: 'We had been on court for half an hour. It was one game all and we'd just started the third,' remembers Jonah. 'In the first game I had been given the inevitable lesson, in the second I began to find my feet a little bit and sensed that Naz was beginning to struggle, not only because of his age but also because he was terribly arthritic as well. Naz suddenly said, "I have seen enough," and left me to pick up the ball. I hadn't the faintest idea what he really thought.'

But what Nasrullah Khan had seen was enough to tell him that the young man who had waited so long to become his pupil was worthy of his attention. He had a seemingly infinite capacity to keep the ball in play, a devastating lack of knowledge about the game and its technique, but a determination to battle. 'He knew I wouldn't rest until I was the best player in the world. I'm not sure whether he believed it was possible at first, but what he did know for certain was that, for the first time in his life, he had in his hands naked ambition with ability to match.'

Nasrullah began to explain technique and to teach Jonah an appreciation of tactics. During lunch and afternoon tea, cutlery would be manoeuvred around the table to illustrate tactics, and from these early conversations a friendship developed that, ironically, some years later, was to be the cause of their parting. Nasrullah was a kindly man and he had the proud bearing and dignity of the unconquerable Pathans. But he was also a lonely man who had not seen his wife and sons in Pakistan for many years. Jonah was to become a son to him, something that, at the time, Mike Corby saw as almost inevitable: 'It was the meeting of two lonely souls. Naz befriended people because he had nobody here. He lived in a little room at the Lansdowne so that anyone who spent any time there got to know him. Jonah was exactly the same, a lost spirit, he had no one.'

Not lacking in perception, Jonah was aware of the intense nature of their relationship and for a long time he enjoyed the warmth that only a true friendship can produce. 'He did look upon me as a son. His attitude was that my family was his family. He was terribly fond of Geraldine and Nicholas and was delighted by my parents whom he met when we went down to Cornwall together. The first time he met my father, my father said, "You are a Pathan". My father knew the Pathans and respected them as he had at one time been stationed on the North-West Frontier. My father offered him a whisky and soda and they got on terribly well. Naz demanded of me the same sort of loyalty that he would have demanded of his own children. I was to show him absolute respect and defer to him all the time. At the word of command I had to jump – and I did because I totally and utterly respected him. I was drawn to him because I sensed that he was very much a part of the great era of the 'fifties, even though he had never been world champion himself.'

Nasrullah knew that with Jonah he would not be able to reproduce a player of Roshan's dazzling skills, but he was aware that if Jonah could develop a physique able to withstand the demands made on it by his fantastic determination to succeed, then a player would emerge capable of buckling the opposition's knees. This was the strategy decided upon by Nasrullah and Jonah was commanded to 'devil up your muscles'. 'One of the things Nasrullah wanted me to do was run, which I was doing anyway, but with a long stride. This is not something which would be advised by the average athletics coach, but what he had in mind was the way one moves on the court with a long last stride to the ball. When I went back home to Marratons I had a regular routine in which I would do sit-ups, press-ups and chin-ups on the branch of a tree, followed by long strides round and round the garden. Nasrullah sensed that I would need tremendous all-round fitness, and it was he who guided me to the weights as he had clients at the Lansdowne who had benefited enormously from weight-training. In fact, he persuaded one or two of them to sponsor my weight-training course at the old Mayfair Gym. I was running, weight-training, practising on court, "devilling" up my muscles – it was a simple system, he had not itemised it nor produced a coaching manual of his own, but the guts of it were right. What's more he knew there had to be an awful lot of work on court and he made me practise by myself because it required fundamental self-discipline. Common sense was inherent in Nasrullah's coaching. For example he would not let me play for four or five days before a championship. "You must be hungry like a lion without a good meal," he would say. So that by the time I went on court I'd be scavenging away. There's so much more to coaching than merely teaching someone how to hit the ball.'

The ball still has to be struck, however, and to an area of the court where it will cause maximum stress and embarrassment to one's opponent. Because of his arthritic knees, Nasrullah was never able to provide Jonah with a consistent, practical demonstration of match play and thus force him to think under pressure. Michael Oddy recognised this and recommended that Jonah played the great Azam Khan. Never one to turn a deaf ear to wise counsel, Jonah readily accepted Oddy's advice and arranged to play Azam during the spring and autumn of 1966. Azam, in retirement, had turned to running the New Grampians squash club deep in the bowels of the earth beneath Shepherd's Bush, and it was from this subterranean redoubt that he continued to dispense a unique wisdom to anyone prepared to listen.

Strange things happen when one is on a squash court with Azam Khan. Undermined, in every way, in an incredibly short space of time, you wonder whether brain and body will ever function in harmony again. Only if you show the strength of character to come back for more will Azam offer advice; others are expected to learn from his example. A dignified man, he is scornful of those who have had an easy ride or who seek one; yet he is still a kindly man. He looks like a sparrow after a bountiful summer, has the courage of a bear, and on the squash court possesses the sharply honed reflexes of a fencing master. Stories of his prowess on court are legion and one pupil, Don Stewart, now a teaching professional, remembers that in his first lesson with Azam the master's racket-head was secured to the shaft with insulating tape and he received service left-handed while blowing his nose. Asked if he was ready to receive service Azam nodded and when the serve arrived – and it was a good serve – it was cut into the nick with such aplomb that Stewart was quite convinced that Azam was left-handed.

In the spring of 1966, then, Jonah set off for Shepherd's Bush and the first of many daily meetings with Azam. 'I used to play Azam in the mornings, and although morning games have always been difficult for me, this was something else. I was literally put on the rack – in fact I can never remember playing Azam without getting into some kind of physical distress. It was a strange experience as I was supposed to be hot stuff, yet here was this little man, well over forty, putting me through the wringer. He hadn't played competitively for four years and in that time he had torn his achilles tendon, dislocated his wrist and generally aged – yet he could still make me look and feel like a village idiot.'

Azam, whose only losing battle has been against the inconsistencies of the English language, gleefully recalls making a mug of the young Barrington, who might have been a leading British player, but to him was only a beginner and a raw one at that. 'He was no good with racket when he came here. He was not natural player. I give you ideas of his standard when he came here. He left-handed and left-hander do very long swing and once he hit me with racket. Only bad player or bad man hit you with racket. He hit me in teeth and make one loose, it still black, and in the eye, it was cut . . . I say to him "Jonah, you don't have to do this to me." He got very upset on court if losing or not doing well. I tell him, keep calm, be patient to be world champion, keep on trying. We had 45-minute court first thing in morning, 20, 25 minute he leave court, too tired, he not fit then. I say "Jonah, you got to keep on trying."'

By playing Azam, Jonah quickly learned where not to hit the ball, how to defend under pressure, and of course how to punish his opponents:

Azam's rallying was all precision and he had a very calm brain, it was as if he had it all charted. He was like a computer in the way he would produce his strokes and construct a rally. He always eschewed the spectacular for the efficient placement and yet he could fire the ball into the nick at will. He felt that under championship conditions it was better to contain one's opponent close to the side walls. The actual practical demonstration of precision squash was absolutely unbelievable – all done without the over-use of energy or a hint of the spectacular.

He moved around so silently that one was never aware of where he was. He didn't follow the modern trend of banging the foot in the stroke. It seemed that whatever shot I played he would anticipate it; if I hit a cross-court he would be on to it tremendously fast and I knew I would have to pay for my indiscretion. With a quick dart of the arm and a quick movement of the body, the ball would be despatched to a difficult area of the court. He would do this again and again.

I was fully aware that I was receiving a tremendously graphic lesson as to why the ball had to be played accurately; because if the ball was a fraction out from the side wall Azam would volley it dead. And what was psychologically alarming was that, very often, he would play his shot and out of the corner of my eye I would see him take his handkerchief out of his pocket and start mopping his brow as he continued to play the rally.

Thus Jonah toiled away in Shepherd's Bush under Azam and at the Lansdowne under Nasrullah, improving almost by the minute. Reconciled to the fact that Azam was from another squash planet altogether, Jonah was much encouraged by the ease with which he was now regularly beating his other practice partners. 'I would go back to the Lansdowne and in the afternoon play somebody like Jonathan Smith, the England international, and crucify him. Although Jonathan was a very good player the difference between him and Azam was chalk and cheese.'

For the rest of the year, Jonah continued to beaver away and in the traditional curtain-raiser of the new season he slaughtered Jeremy Lyon in the Strawson Memorial Match. Suddenly it was December and the British Open was upon him. Seeded No 5, Jonah knew that if things went according to plan, he would have to play the great Abou Taleb in the quarter-finals.

Taleb, an Egyptian, had rocketed through the ranks from obscurity with a type of squash so spectacular that it could only be played by a man whose racket is an extension of his arm. He was a wizard, the Muhammad Ali of squash, and the knowing ones gave Jonah no chance at all of beating him. But before he could prove them wrong it was necessary to overcome Mike Corby who had been stung into organising his own game by suggestions that Jonah had overtaken him. Jonah won a hard match 9–5, 7–9, 9–7, 9–4 and the confrontation with Taleb was on. But it very nearly wasn't. Forgetting Naz's advice, Jonah had played practice matches with Azam up until the start of the championship and had been demolished in straight games on six consecutive days. This mortifying experience had triggered such a depression in Jonah that he wanted to withdraw from the competition:

I was really down in the dumps and told Azam that, as I had hardly taken a point off him all week, let alone a game, what was the use of me playing when he was at least twenty years older than me and still able to destroy me? 'Don't be silly,' said Azam. 'I know the people who is winning this Open. You just keep running and you will beat them. I know their standard, you just keep running and get the ball back. You win, you see. You do what I tell you, you play your game, you see what happen.'

He had seen Taleb playing in his club in the week before the championship against Ali Ispahani who was a very good player. The gallery was packed with club members who wanted to marvel at the skills of the great Taleb, who did not disappoint them as he produced one dazzling stroke after another. Azam's members were awestruck and said no wonder Taleb is world champion. Azam, not wishing to argue with his members, agreed. What he did not tell them was that with his practised eye he had noticed that when Taleb was taken to the front of the court his movement was reasonable but that in returning to the centre he sometimes had to push off the front wall to get back.

Nasrullah also kept a close eye on Taleb and he knew that his waist had gone up three inches from the previous year (Naz was very friendly with the Fred Perry people who had told him that Taleb was now taking a larger size of shorts). Azam and Nazrullah fed me a list of Taleb's weaknesses and they convinced me that I was going to beat him. They even managed to convince me that my ball control was very nearly the same standard as his. Azam even told me how the match would go. 'He play winner, you return winner. He play winner again, you return winner again – Taleb hit tin, that will happen.' And, my oath, it *did* happen.

I had a bad night's sleep before the match, my mind preying on the fact that Taleb had not been beaten for four years. Before the match Taleb had told the boys on reception at the Lansdowne that he was going to put me out of my misery early on. When the knock-up started he played to the gallery using all his exhibition shots, playing behind his back, between his legs, etc. The gallery was laughing, cheering and clapping, but I kept my head down because Nazrullah had warned me not to show any emotion.

When the game began he went on playing in the same cavalier fashion but I got away to an early lead and took the first game 9–4. I took the second game 9–1 and then he really started his tricks. He began turning the ball and drilling me with it, he hit me with his racket and knocked me over, and in between all these terrorist tactics he switched on to playing championship squash. He took the third game 10–8 and I was suddenly desperate. Then I hit one of my rare non-percentage shots. It was a backhand volleyed drop shot from the back of the service box off what appeared to be a perfect Taleb drive. I was now back in control and won the fourth game 9–5 after Taleb had asked for a let on match point. I had played a drop and it wasn't a particularly good one and I felt that Taleb could have got to it. Nazrullah, who was marking, did not even bother to refer to the referee and barked 'no let' and the place erupted.

(Some may find it strange that Jonah's coach was marking the match, but in 1966 there was still some honour left in squash and it would not have been thought exceptional in any way.)

In his report, Rex Bellamy, writing in *The Times* the following day, said that the game had been

a dazzling exhibition of technique and tactics within the framework of a brawl, in which Barrington had to take everything except punches. He finished with three bruises on the back and one on the jaw, three of them showing blood.

Moreover, Taleb three times asked for a respite, twice to change his trousers, once to fetch a handkerchief. What with this, and the repeated occasions when he was struck by shoulder, ball or racket, Barrington must have thought that Taleb was trying everything he knew to break the Cornishman's spirit and concentration.

It was the combination of all these factors that made Barrington's such a glorious triumph. First, he proved that he could beat Taleb at squash. Then he proved that his courage and concentration could withstand a multitude of distractions, not the least of them physical intimidation.

As in last season's final against Jawaid, Taleb's fine squash was marred by court manners that brought no credit to the professional game. This cast a cloud over what was basically a superb match, disputed at a furious pace – yet with Barrington time and time again deceiving a man we had regarded as the crown prince of deceivers.

All Taleb's wizardry – notably his inimitable use of the reverse angle – came to nothing. Barrington read him like an open book and himself played masterful squash, mixing the long and the short games with acuteness and control. The shot of the match was Barrington's – a winning volleyed drop from a shot of Taleb's that looked an irretrievable length down Barrington's backhand.

The great thing was that in every way – courage, skill, and the ability to produce a winning shot when it mattered – Barrington was Taleb's master. The game as a whole, and the British game in particular, will be all the better for it.

Mike Corby was in the gallery and marvelled at the dignity Jonah displayed in the face of this violent assault: 'Everybody knew that, in a scrap, Taleb would get dirty, and what everyone admired was the way Jonah beat him, the way he was hit fifteen times with the ball and didn't react. In my view Jonah was playing a part, creating a myth. The more he was hit the less he reacted. It was the start of the legend. He held himself together and he was sensationally good.'

After the match – the match that made him a star – Jonah sat by himself on the stairs savouring his achievement but remembering with sadness his father who had died of cancer that November and had not lived to see his wayward son's first, important triumph.

Having only played the game seriously for a little over two years, the pressure was really on Jonah now that he had knocked out the invincible Taleb. But he was on a winning streak and, like all good gamblers, he rode his luck. Another Egyptian, Ibrahim Amin, a strokeplayer almost in the Taleb class but nine years older than Jonah, was eclipsed 9–4, 4–9, 9–5, 9–3 in the semi-final, and Jonah was through to the final and a meeting with the inscrutable Pakistani, Aftab Jawaid, three times British Amateur champion.

Jawaid arrived at the final short of competition with only three matches behind him, having spent four days in bed with 'flu. But he had played a 100-minute semi-final against Mo Yasin which was enough to suggest that he was on the mend. Also, he was a vastly experienced performer whose forte was seducing his opponents into playing his type of game – driving endlessly down the side walls to a length, which he did better than anyone else. Nasrullah was well aware of this but he also knew that Jawaid was appallingly weak for a player of his class on the volley above shoulder height, especially on the backhand, and it was this weakness that Jonah was instructed to exploit.

From the outset, Jonah made telling use of the lob to Jawaid's backhand and only in the second game was he lulled into an hypnotic exchange of driving down the walls. He won the match 9–2, 6–9, 9–2, 9–2, and hit twenty-four winners. His most telling stroke was the backhand drop shot and when Jawaid began to anticipate this Jonah had the wit to use the forehand drop more often or with a late flick of the wrist turn his backhand drop across court.

The success that Jonah had craved for most of his young life was now his. He had finally put behind him the black days of Cheltenham, the roistering of Trinity and achieved something in the face of difficulties both real and imagined. How did he celebrate his breakthrough? Rex Bellamy wrote in *The Times* that 'the champagne was flowing in Berkeley Square' – it was, but not into Jonah's glass. The paranoia was already beginning to emerge. 'There was always a problem celebrating after my finals, even after the first one. I felt very irritable because everyone was crawling around trying to organise things. I felt they were all trying to derive something from my victory. Once the formalities had been completed I didn't want to say much to anyone, I just wanted to dwell on the satisfaction in private, but there were all these people circling around in search of a share of what had happened. The effort had been made and nobody, not even my coach, could ever have appreciated what had gone into it. I enjoyed the privacy of the shower because that was the one place where I could dwell on my achievement, but as soon as I emerged I would be public property again and surrounded by all the clamour. On the one hand I resented all the fuss straight afterwards, and on the other hand I resented the lack of attention the following day when there would be absolutely nothing.'

Three weeks later in January 1967 Jonah had to gear himself to meet a new challenge. It was time for the British Amateur championship and news of his Open triumph had filtered through to Australia where Kenny Hiscoe and Dick Carter were preparing to put the upstart in his place. Hiscoe, awesomely positive and master of the backhand volley and boast, was Jonah's semi-final opponent.

For two-and-a-half games Jonah was terribly loose, pushing the ball instead of hitting it and leaving Hiscoe too many opportunities on the volley in mid-court. He quickly found himself two games down with Hiscoe leading at 5–4 in the third. This was the crisis and Hiscoe was still playing well, but suddenly Jonah began to strike the ball more positively, rediscovering his accuracy. Now the ball was hugging the side walls, denying Hiscoe the opportunity to make his devastating mid-court interceptions. Jonah began to mix the long and short games and Hiscoe's thirteen stone was having to cover more of the court. Jonah weathered the storm and took the very tense third game, 9–5, in twenty-four minutes.

However, there was still enough bounce left in Hiscoe's legs to take him to a 3–0 lead in the fourth. His boasts had never been better but Jonah was onto them in an instant, playing a mixture of drops and drives, and soon his challenger was being stranded by yards. In the fifth the court had assumed such huge dimensions that Hiscoe simply couldn't cover it. Jonah produced a string of drop shots and Hiscoe's challenge evaporated after eight minutes. It was a glorious spectacle for the gallery who were unaccustomed to seeing Australians buckle at the knees.

If only Jonah could beat Dick Carter in the final he would become only the second person ever to achieve the double of Open and Amateur in the same season since the aristocratic Egyptian, Amr Bey, had first performed the feat in 1932.

With Dick Carter leading him by 2–1 and 7–4 in the fourth it did not look as though Jonah was going to succeed. Carter had used the side walls intelligently to draw Jonah to the front of the court where he had been strangely hesitant on the drop shot. He wasn't just clipping the tin, he was hitting the bottom of it. But at 7–4 Carter made a strange error and wasn't to score another point. He went for a relatively easy backhand volley with the whole of the court open to him but hit the tin. Jonah swept through to level the match. At the brief interval, Nicholas Barrington and Nasrullah repaired to the bar for a drop of the hard stuff, in anticipation of a long, gruelling final game. As it turned out, someone looked in almost immediately and told them Jonah was about to win the match. Whereas the first four games had taken ninety-three minutes, the fifth was over in less than four. Dreadfully tired, Carter made a series of errors and looked incapable of playing out a rally. Jonah hit four winners and for the second time in a week the gallery witnessed the unusual spectacle of an Australian crumpling at the knees.

The miracle had happened, but Jonah was then faced

with the dilemma well known to all miracle-workers – how to follow that? The World Amateur Championship was to be held in Australia in the autumn and Jonah would have to begin careful preparation. He was captain of the British team and No 1 seed for the individual title, with a much-relished confrontation ahead with Geoff Hunt in the final. But, despite all of this, it was to be a desperately disappointing trip for Jonah and one in which his inexperience showed.

Unaccustomed to long-distance air travel instead of resting and taking things easy and acclimatising himself gradually, Jonah went straight into training on arrival. Jet-lag immediately caught up with him. In his first two matches for the British team, against New South Wales and another selected side, he was beaten 3–0 by Cam Nancarrow in eighteen minutes in one with Kenny Hiscoe taking a minute longer to beat him 3–0 in the other. So confused was Jonah, not just by the effects of long-distance travel but also by the mysteries of the Australian ball, that he was even losing to his team mates in practice. Applying himself with determination, he gained some measure of confidence by winning the Queensland championship and, in the World Amateur team event, he won each of his matches against Pakistan, South Africa and New Zealand before losing 9–5 to Hiscoe in the fifth in the match against Australia. 'I had a two-sets-to-love lead and was ahead in the third but Kenny fought his way out of it. I was a little over-confident at that stage mainly because I was so relieved that I was not only in contention but actually seemed to have him in some difficulty. It was a very close match and there were some appreciative comments. I felt I had shown the crowd something of the real Jonah Barrington and began to feel more confident about my chances in the individual event.'

Playing reasonably well, Jonah beat the South African Dawie Botha in the quarter-final to earn a place in the semis against Cam Nancarrow. But the Australians believed that Barrington's Open and Amateur victories were something of a fluke and were absolutely determined that he should not walk off with the first official world title, especially as it was being held on their own soil. 'We felt Jonah played too loose,' said Kenny Hiscoe. 'He wanted to bury us in the back of the court all the time so we decided to play him in the front of the court where we thought we could easily read his intentions.'

This was to be Jonah's second meeting with Nancarrow, the man who was to become his bogey. Two years earlier they had played each other in London as reserves in a match between Britain and Australia – Jonah had won, and he was expected to win again as he was now the *de facto* world champion. But champions are made to fall and, sadly, he came crashing down, a victim of Nancarrow's bullet drives and feathered drop shots. Jonah was beaten 9–7, 9–6, 9–7 and, apart from praising him for saving five match points, the Australian press and public rubbed salt into his wounds with a relish rarely found in other parts of the world. 'I was terribly dejected. I had gone out to Australia to prove I was the best player in the world and I hadn't done it. I had a bottle of champagne that somebody had given me in the dressing room which was ready to be opened when I won the final, but here I was knocked out in the semis. I was sorely tempted to drink it but instead I poured it down the drain. Perhaps it would have been better if I *had* drunk it.'

Mike Corby remembers Jonah's black despair immediately after the Nancarrow defeat and the measures he employed to try to snap his captain out of it: 'I was in the showers with Jonah and he started crying, so I hit him. I said, "you're captain of my team and no bloody captain of mine starts crying – you got beaten and that's the end of it. People will look at you more in defeat than in victory, never forget that." I think he understood – I think he appreciated what I was saying.'

Traumatic though that 1967 Australian tour was for Barrington, the trip did provide one massive consolation – he met Aub Amos. By any standards, Amos was a remarkable man. A former winner of the Australian Open Judo Championships, Amos did not come across the game of squash until he was in his thirties and he fell in love with the sport. And his involvement with squash has virtually covered every sphere of the game. He has won a number of veteran titles including the Australian Championships, he has served as an administrator, he created his own squash complex, he served as an advisor to Slazengers on rackets and balls and he is heavily involved in youth coaching programmes.

Barrington first met Amos at a Queensland Association dinner when officials were trying to persuade the troubled Cornishman to visit, of all places, a pineapple factory, when all he wanted was a complete rest from the pressures of the tour. 'Ah, shit, give the guy a break,' said a middle-aged man interrupting the conversation. And Barrington and Amos later became great friends.

Other people such as Jonah's father, his schoolteacher Jack Sweetman and his coach Nasrullah Khan may have had a more obvious influence on Barrington's life. But in Jonah's mind, Aub Amos has been a crucial figure in his life:

> Aub Amos is one of the most remarkable characters I have ever met. He has the most enormous amount of natural energy. His life has been a never ending saga of 'experiences' and he is an astonishing raconteur. He is also a very shrewd businessman with the mental capacity to handle practical problems.
>
> I had nothing but aggravation on that tour. I had been given too much responsibility and the reason I finally played reasonably well was that Aub helped me out. Later his influence was vital. He had been down life's dry gullies and he knew the shortcuts. When I came along, he couldn't believe how naive I was. He showed me how I could avoid being taken for a ride by the games promoters and businessmen. He taught me how to look after my own welfare. I haven't come across anyone who knows more about the game of squash in *all* its aspects.

But for Amos, Barrington might have become involved in a questionable business venture to build a series of Jonah Barrington squash court complexes in Britain. Amos attended the business meeting in which various people tried to persuade Jonah that these expensive complexes could be built with a minimum outlay – others could be found to provide the funds. 'You're talking a load of bullshit,' said Amos bluntly. And the complexes were never built because no effective answer was provided when the Australian pinpointed the practical deficiencies of the grandiose scheme.

On his arrival in England, Jonah planned a campaign that, if successful, would make him indisputably the world No 1. He set himself the Herculean task of winning nine major championships – the British Open in December 1967, the British Amateur in January 1968, the Egyptian Open in March, the South African Amateur Championship in July and the Australian Amateur in late August. These would be followed by the British Open and Amateur again, the World Amateur team championships and finally the World Amateur individual title in February 1969.

In Australia in 1967 Barrington had not done justice to himself. The responsibility of handling the British team was too much for him – others in the party were far senior to him, he lacked the experience needed for the task and he was unaware of the problems posed by the Australian ball and acclimatisation. But Barrington had learnt from his mistakes. Free from the responsibility of guiding others as well as himself, he now began knocking off those championships one by one. He won the British Open, beating Taleb 3–0 in the final, and then the British Amateur with a 3–1 victory against Mike Corby. Then he won the Egyptian Open, beating Taleb again, 9–4, 9–2, 9–7, on his home court before a packed gallery at the Heliopolis Sporting Club in Cairo. Then came the South African title without conceding a game. Then it was back to Australia where a more experienced, wiser Jonah was determined to show the Australian public just what he could do.

I roared straight into the semi-finals of the Australian Championships without dropping a set and beat Dick Carter in the quarter-final for the loss of only about nine points, which was highly satisfying.

My opponent in the semi-final was Geoff Hunt, and I found myself in the strange position of being two games ahead with a lead in the third. It looked as if I was going through to the final without dropping a set, but of course it was too good to last. He came storming back at me. Hunt always comes at you again and again, he never gives in and you can never assume he's finished. In that match he came from the brink of defeat to two games all but I just managed to edge him 9–6 in the fifth.

Then, having hardly recovered, I had to take on a very fresh and determined Hiscoe in the final the following day but, after a long, hard match, he ran out of steam and I beat him 9–1 in the fifth. Having now beaten Carter, Hiscoe and Hunt on their own soil I really did feel that I had silenced my Australian critics and justified my reputation.

Back home again, the British Amateur was duly accounted for when Jonah beat Mike Corby 3–1 in an excellent final.

It had been a marvellous year for Jonah and he was unquestionably on top of the world. But ironically, having silenced his critics, far from enjoying his unchallenged superiority he found the new responsibility of being world champion an enormous burden. Just when he needed to adopt a positive attitude with the World Team and Individual Championships coming up, his confidence began to drain away. Fully aware that so much was expected of him, he completely flopped in the British Open and crashed out 4–9, 5–9, 8–10 to Cam Nancarrow in the semi-final. It was a desperately insecure Jonah who then had to get mentally ready for the World Team Championships and the Individual title. 'I struggled through the team series and had the dreadful experience of having to save a match point in the fifth against Jawaid that would have cost us the whole match against Pakistan. But then I drew encouragement from beating Geoff Hunt 9–7 in the fifth in the match against Australia and this made me feel a little more confident as I was sure Hunt would be my opponent if I got through to the final of the individual event.'

Jonah had decided that, win or lose, he was going to turn professional after the final of the World Amateur championship and he had geared the last eighteen months of effort with this in mind. He would have turned professional in 1967 had he won the World title in Australia, but Nancarrow had fouled things up for him. Now, however, in the World Amateur event, he had the satisfaction of avenging his 1967 defeat when he finally laid the Nancarrow bogey by beating him 3–0 to win a place in the final against Hunt.

Despite losing the first game against Hunt, from a good lead, Jonah took the second 9–2 and was about 3–0 up in the third and nicely on the path to victory when suddenly he felt drained of energy and lost concentration. Simultaneously, Hunt had begun to play in his most disciplined manner. 'Geoff was probably thinking to himself that if he was going to lose he wasn't going to give me the match on a plate. He was determined not to make a single mistake – and he didn't. But instead of keeping calm in the fourth I panicked and tried to hit the rubber off the ball, which isn't really my game, and almost as a punishment I didn't score a single point. I had blown at a critical stage in the match and I just couldn't find the concentration to calm down and play my way back in.'

His well-laid plans to turn professional in a blaze of glory as world champion were shattered and Jonah regards that loss to Hunt as his bitterest defeat. 'What more could I have done? I couldn't have trained harder. If I had been able to look at it objectively afterwards I would have realised that there was little between us on the day, but all I knew was that I had lost a vital match that had built up in my mind for eighteen months and I felt a grievous sense of injustice. Nobody seemed to share my disappointment and as far as I could see the other players couldn't give a monkey's. I was totally dejected and I couldn't sleep. So, in the early hours of the morning I wandered around London, feeling utterly confused. Losing to Nancarrow was pretty horrifying but this was even worse – the world had dropped from under my feet.'

The following day Jonah duly gave his press conference at the Lansdowne and announced that he was turning professional. He then flew off to South Africa where the warm climate and the change of environment were to heal his wounds and where he could begin to sort out his professional career.

Since the summer of 1966 Jonah had strictly speaking been a 'shamateur', receiving under-the-counter payments from various backers, and although these sums were enough income to keep body and soul together, they didn't constitute anywhere near enough to plan for the future. But having achieved the double of British Open and Amateur in the 1966 season, the rest of the world demanded to see him play, and everywhere he went his expenses were met in full. This was a pleasant state of affairs for a young athlete who had never liked getting up in the morning but at the end of the day it didn't provide any capital. Pondering this problem carefully while lying on a beach in South Africa, he came up with the revolutionary idea of touring Britain with Geoff Hunt in a fifteen-match exhibition series and charging for admission. The scheme seemed perfect and, additionally, it would give him the opportunity of playing his fiercest rival under match-play conditions. In spite of tremendous opposition from the Australian and British SRAs, who were concerned about Hunt's amateur status, the tour got under way. On the playing side it was a calamity for Jonah because he lost the series 13–2, and financially it was hardly a success either, with the amateur Hunt receiving his maximum £8 per day allowance and Jonah paying Geoff's and his wife's return fare from Australia.

Nevertheless the timing of the tour meant that Geoff would be in England for the 1969 Open and I knew that with him participating, it would regain its former status as the world's leading tournament.

I trained harder than I had ever trained before in preparing for his visit and I was in terrific shape both mentally and physically, although perhaps a little short of competition. But I was in for another rude awakening. He destroyed me in forty minutes 3–0 in the first match in Coventry, and won the next two as well. Then, four days before the Open was due to start, we played at Wolverhampton.

We were about eight-all in the third after about an hour and ten minutes when I broke what must have been my seventh racket that week and had to borrow one from the Australian bloke who was driving us around. I was so exasperated that Geoff served nine times and I hit the tin nine times, and even the floor; so I cleared off the court. The club was very annoyed and didn't want to pay us the money as they thought they hadn't had full value. My agent, then Clive Everton, told them they had seen better squash than they were ever likely to and that they had no appreciation of the situation. But despite that, I shouldn't have done what I did. However, I knew that I would have had to play for another hour to win that match and that would have taken too much out of me before the start of the Open.

And Jonah was not wrong. But even with his insight he could not have foreseen that, in the final of the 1969 Open, he and Hunt would play each other for two hours and thirteen minutes, and thus establish a new world record, before Jonah lurched home victorious 9–4 in the fifth. So frustrated was Hunt by this defeat that he pounded out another nine wins over Jonah in their exhibition series, producing a spectacular quality of play night after night. 'His consistently high quality was a miracle and so I had to accept that for the rest of my career my main target would always have to be the British Open. All my resources would have to be gathered for that because I knew that, if Hunt was playing, it would need boundless mental resources and a prodigious physical performance on my part to beat him.'

Many people have wondered how Jonah managed to beat Hunt so convincingly in all those major finals yet lose so comprehensively to him in their exhibition series. Kenny Hiscoe, who knows both men well and Hunt better than most, gives a clue: 'Nobody, not even Hashim Khan, could produce the same high quality as Geoff could night after night – he was a machine. Jonah was more like Lew Hoad in tennis who would get it all together for the big one – which, of course, is the one that counts.'

Jonah went on winning the big one. He beat Aftab Jawaid 9–1, 9–2, 9–6, in the 1970 British Open, beat Hunt again in 1972, 0–9, 9–7, 10–8, 6–9, 9–7, and achieved his last victory in the Open in 1973 by beating Gogi Alauddin 9–4, 9–3, 9–2. As far as Jonah was concerned he had a score to settle with Gogi and was absolutely determined to beat him.

Gogi and I had played a round-robin affair with Hiscoe and Hunt all over Australia. The prize money was awarded on a basis of games won and Hunt, who by that time could have beaten Hiscoe 3–0 at will, had been giving Hiscoe games. So I gave Gogi games from which he earned a few hundred pounds more than he would otherwise have done. But from his behaviour towards me, he seemed to have forgotten this and so I decided to teach him a lesson.

It was a wonderful match to play and only lasted about forty minutes because it was just one of those days when everything I did worked perfectly. I'd pick the spot and the ball would go there. It was one of the few occasions in my career when I had the feeling that I was playing out of my mind. The funny thing about it was that I hadn't really wanted to play because I'd picked up an infection and was feeling pretty lousy, but after taking some medicine I upped and turned on one of my best performances.

Jonah could never allow himself the luxury of relaxing in spite of his domination of the British Open, and with Hunt around there was no chance of becoming big-headed. But what of Nasrullah Khan, the man so central to Jonah's success? While revelling in Jonah's achievements, he was beginning to feel resentful that he was being neglected. But such feelings were totally ill-founded: it was just that since Jonah's triumphs in 1966 he had been travelling the world, unable to see Naz on a daily basis. And in all honesty he was thoroughly enjoying his new-found freedom.

Such freedom was a novel experience for Jonah. In the early days with Naz, Jonah had regularly trained so demonically that there were times when exhaustion dictated a temporary respite from his coach's inflexible regime. Still bitterly aware of what he considered to be Roshan's errors in that area, Nasrullah found the idea of Jonah having a girl-friend anathema. Rex Bellamy described their partnership as the meeting of two civilisations, East and West. If that was the case, then it was Jonah and not Nasrullah who was living the life of an orthodox Muslim. No drinking, no smoking and above all no women were to be the cornerstones of Jonah's existence – as Nasrullah wanted him to lead it.

It was not until 1972 that Nasrullah was to see Jonah take a drink; smoking has never provided a temptation and as for girlfriends, Jonah's appetite has never been any different from the next man's. But between 1965 and 1967 he quite deliberately eschewed the temptations:

> I was sharing a flat with a number of friends, all of them lusty lads with girl friends. I think they must have considered me to be very strange. I can remember a girl in the flat below making a beeline for me – she was a bit of a character. I liked her, too. But Nasrullah believed in absolute concentration on the task in hand and, according to him, there was definitely no time for social life. Any attachment to a girl was seen as the inevitable road to disaster. Naz had a terrible hang-up about sexual intercourse – he believed it weakened and destroyed the knees! He'd tell me at great length about how Roshan had broken down in the knees quite shortly after having been British Open champion. He could not comprehend that Roshan simply had an arthritic condition in his knees. If he so much as saw me talking to a girl at the Lansdowne you could guarantee that all I would have to do was look up and there he'd be, glaring at me from the other side of the swimming pool. That glare told me everything.

Nasrullah's insistence that Jonah should be the only monk living in the West End of London was a major reason for the inevitable deterioration of their friendship. That Jonah worked so hard for so long was only due to the fact that he had immense respect for Nasrullah and his methods. He was after all winning championships, and his hunger for victory and the immense satisfaction of achieving it probably outweighed his other desires. But never to the extent that Jonah could absent himself from the company of women completely. However, Nasrullah would always find out somehow and the inevitable clash would follow. 'The worst run-in came after a considerable spell of celibacy when I met a girl who was at Nottingham University – Nancy. She really was smashing. One day, in some trepidation, I took her to the Lansdowne to watch me play Denis Hughes. She was the only person in the gallery but, in the middle of the game, I looked up and saw Nasrullah sitting next to her and they were both chatting away. "Great", I thought, "terrific, they're getting on." I overcame Denis in a tight five and when I went up to her after the game she gave me the elbow! Apparently Naz had explained to her that if the relationship continued my concentration would go and it would be the end of my career. I don't think he actually told her that my knees would rot but he had certainly convinced her that if my career so much as faltered she would never forgive herself. So that was the end of Nancy. I was very angry. It was the first time I had ever been so angry with Nasrullah. I had been irritable before but now I was enraged. For a couple of days afterwards I wouldn't talk to him, but he knew, he just waited and then inevitably we talked.'

And when they did talk Nasrullah explained that Jonah would not be able to fulfil his ambitions unless there was total concentration on the task in hand. Everything that distracted him made him less psychologically strong and weaker in the eyes of the opposition. Nasrullah exhorted him never to have chinks in his armour, never to be seen to be weak, never to show an opponent a weakness, never to let an opponent see fatigue – 'Take a deep breath in the front of the court but never show fatigue'.

The fact that Jonah was able to withstand a daily dose of this advice only emphasises his remarkable strength of character. His later trips abroad removed him from the dissecting gaze both of Nasrullah and his sister Geraldine who had come to believe that Naz knew just what was best for her brother. 'Geraldine and Naz made life very difficult for me, and looking back I believe that Geraldine was terribly jealous. I can recall that whenever she had an inkling that I might possibly be having a relationship with a girl she knew, not necessarily a friend of hers, but even a friend of a friend, it really put her hackles up. One day I suddenly realised it would not be the most sensible thing to let her know that I was nipping in and out of bed with this bird. She wouldn't have approved because she knew that Nasrullah would be furious. Between them they were isolating me from people other than themselves – I was not allowed to have anything.'

But despite their battles, Jonah will always be aware of the enormous contribution that Nasrullah made to his career. So, too, is his brother, Nicholas: 'Jonah always had the *desire* to win but Nasrullah showed him *how* to win. When it gets to eight-all in the fifth some people win games and some don't. Jonah went through a period of ten years when he would win from those crisis situations. Azam would claim that he taught Jonah how to play and, indeed, from playing Azam, Jonah realised that if he hit the ball a half an inch from the wall, his opponent would hit it into the nick. Naz couldn't do that because he couldn't move freely but he knew how to drive Jonah on day after day. I would give Azam great credit but Naz the greater credit for what my brother achieved.'

7. *The Great Rivals*

The contrast between Geoff Hunt and Jonah Barrington, both as men and players, could hardly have been greater. Nevertheless they did share something in common and that was a pathological hatred of losing. Because of this their battles for the major titles produced some of the most dramatic squash ever seen. Their rivalry was every bit as compelling as an Ali–Frazier fight, a Coe–Ovett race or a Borg–Connors tennis match, with their supporters equally divided over the respective merits of each player.

Yet ironically, had Hunt not accepted Jonah's advice, he might never have won his record eight British Open titles and be widely regarded as the game's greatest ever player. The Australian's problem was cramp which attacked him in long matches no matter how assiduously he trained to prevent it. An example of this occurred in the fifth set of the 1970 Australian Open final, when he was reduced to receiving service while standing on one leg like a stork. Jonah, astonished by the sight of his stricken opponent, was moved to ask Hunt if he would like a breather – a gesture not perhaps entirely in keeping with his character on court. Hunt declined the offer and Jonah, now faced by an opponent hardly able to move, ran out an easy winner.

Jonah had seen Hunt distressed by cramp before and, in an extraordinary gesture of concern, set out to cure the single chink in the armour of his greatest rival. Who could imagine Muhammad Ali advising Joe Frazier on the best method of avoiding his jab? And Jonah was successful, too, much to the dismay of Nasrullah. 'Never tell them anything, never tell them anything,' was the hard-headed Pathan's attitude to Jonah advising his opponents. 'But here was a great athlete whom I admired,' argues Jonah, 'and he was in a panic. His cooling system was different from everybody else's. While I was charging around getting hotter and hotter, sweating buckets and going purple in the face, Geoff, under the same conditions, would be turning whiter and whiter. I described his condition to Freddie Griffiths, the Manchester City physiotherapist, who said it sounded like a lack of sodium, a quite common condition, and told me to suggest slow-release sodium tablets.'

Jonah's prescription obviously worked as Hunt went on to complete his glittering career untroubled by cramp except when he neglected to take the sodium tablets. He conceded that it was an extraordinary thing for Jonah to have done: 'I don't know why he did it. But the pills certainly worked, though I was a little suspicious at the time as I didn't think Jonah knew too much about the effects of slow-release sodium!'

For more than a decade, Geoff Hunt so dominated Jonah's thoughts that even now he sometimes wakes in the morning quite convinced that he has just played him. Sadly, with Hunt now reduced by arthritis to a state where he can no longer play competitively, this is no longer a possiblity. But now the competition between them is at an end, how do they feel about each other, looking back at a rivalry that illuminated the squash world for more than a decade?

They are not great friends but nevertheless have a close relationship, built principally on mutual respect and admiration. It is the same kind of respect a fighter shows for his opponent after the bout, having spent the previous 45 minutes trying to render him insensible; the kind of feeling that, in retirement, turns to respect, when jealousy, greed for victory and other motivational qualities are suddenly surplus requirements.

Although both men display widely differing virtues as players and human beings, the parallels remain. Both their fathers were physically small men with forceful personalities. Both had an elder brother more naturally gifted at the game. Both possessed the same tremendously disciplined attitude to training and shared a capacity to ignore physical discomfort and pain. Both are certainly highly articulate, Hunt's responses being carefully considered, while Jonah's verbal style is all reflex and imagination.

Jonah well remembers the first time he set eyes on Hunt and the two other Australians who were to become his rivals – Hiscoe and Carter. It was 1965, and Barrington was duplicating reams of paper and borrowing the insurance stamp money at the SRA when the Australians arrived to play in the British Amateur. To put in perspective their respective skills on the squash court, Hunt, then only 17, was to contest the final that year with Jawaid, losing in four sets but without being embarrassed in any area of the court, while Jonah was a front-wall starer trying without success to get into Hampstead Cricket Club's Cumberland Cup squash team. 'I went along to watch them play and practise at the Lansdowne,' remembers Jonah, 'and I can recall the tremendous psychological advantages they had over the British players. They were all suntanned from the Australian summer and terrifically confident. It was known that Dick Carter used to get fit by running through the surf -- and in those days that sort of training was unheard of. The British players felt they simply couldn't beat the Australians. They were very much the front runners at the time, and through Kenny Hiscoe's influence were playing very positive, spectacular squash. Hiscoe and Carter were the team's strong personalities and they did the talking off court. Hunt was the prodigy.'

The potentially great rivals did not, however, speak that year: there was little reason why they should. Barrington was the not very efficient assistant secretary of the SRA and Geoff would have been ranked among the top six players in the world. The following season, however, Jonah reached the quarter-finals of the British Open and was selected for a representative side that played an exhibition match against Australia. Jonah was seeded above Mike Corby, and this meant that his opponent would be Hunt. Jonah was comprehensively destroyed and, to make matters even worse, Corby beat Hiscoe.

Jonah will not easily forget his first match with Hunt: 'He humiliated me in straight games, with me scoring only about three points. I knew that my playing had advanced but with a six-year age-gap between us, there was no way I could ever see myself reaching his level. Everything happened so fast; he volleyed almost anything and rolled me off the court.' It is the strongest testament therefore to Jonah's extraordinary determination that, only a year after his despair at being routed by Hunt, he had won both the British Open and Amateur and was, *de facto*, the champion of the world.

Before he could savour his first victory over Hunt, however, Jonah had to be patient and await the 1967 British tour to Australia and New Zealand. Here he also had to endure a bout of paranoia brought on, generally, by the mysteries of the Australian ball and the antics of the team he captained on that tour, but primarily on account of his defeat by Cam Nancarrow in the semi-finals of the World Amateur Championship, which would otherwise have brought together Hunt and Barrington in the final. 'I went out to the World Amateur to prove I was the best player in the world and I failed,' recalls Jonah. 'Nancarrow beat me 3–0 in the semi-finals. Then we went on to New Zealand and I played two exhibition matches against Hunt in Christchurch and Timaru. In Christchurch, I had him 8–1 in the fifth and he came back and won. I must have had 10 match points yet I still lost.'

Hunt also remembers their match at Christchurch as well, not because of the game particularly, or the quality of play, but on account of the events in the dressing room afterwards where Barrington produced one of his more spectacular post-defeat tantrums. 'Jonah went berserk,' recalls Hunt, a grin clearly registering the amusement the incident had given him at the time. 'He was hurling his rackets across the changing room when the press came in for an interview. He threw them out using the foulest language imaginable and promptly proceeded to do a series of sit-ups and press-ups until he was physically sick. At the time it was the strangest thing I'd ever seen in my life.'

For Barrington, however, his reaction was to some extent understandable. Having spent a year preparing for the final of the World Amateur only to go out in the semi-finals, to have the cup of victory dashed from his lips, was all too much for his nerve ends. Fortunately Jonah calmed down in time for the match the following night in Timaru. Incredibly, he was again leading 8–2 in the fifth only for Hunt to come back at him. This time Jonah clung on:

> I had reduced him to a condition where he was almost unable to hit the ball and yet, as he did so often, he started to come back. He reached 7–8 by which time I was frothing at the mouth and gibbering. I could see exactly the same thing happening again. I hit a nick to get the service back from what I would call a non-percentage situation. I served, we had a rally, I hit a cross court nick and the ball squirted across the floor. I had won and I remember knowing that I had purged my soul. The feeling of elation, even though it was only an exhibition match, was fantastic.
>
> To me, it was so much more than an exhibition match. I had worked so hard for the World Amateur Championship and lost; so even though I was British Open and Amateur Champion I had still not proved I was the best player in the world. Geoff had won the title just a couple of nights before so, to me, those exhibition matches were like the final of the World Championship. They were incredible matches, exceedingly long. The Hunt–Barrington rivalry was now definitely on.

At the time, neither could have known just how great a toll their rivalry was to take of their physical and mental resources. Today we can see the results of their daily commitment to training schedules which, if undertaken by lesser men, would swamp the cardiac treatment resources of the nation's hospitals. The legacy of that relentless grind is that Hunt now has an arthritic hip and is unable even to kick a football with his son, while Jonah has a new back, racket arm, and knee.

Without doubt, it was both players' commitment to training that enabled them to last so long while producing matches of such quality. Defeat would only signal an even greater training load. For Jonah, six years older than Hunt, this was especially hard as he could not let up for a moment. After victory or defeat, he would be up the next day and

The young Cornishman – and the living legend. (On the left) 25-year-old Jonah Barrington practising at the Lansdowne Club in December 1966, just before he shocked the squash world by winning the British Open for the first time. (Above) Barrington in the late '70s after he had become the most famous squash player in the history of the game. The photographs also show how the game has changed – note how different the squash shoes now are, while the transparent back wall in the later picture didn't exist in the mid-'60s

Jonah when he was a student at Trinity College, Dublin, pictured with 'Pilly' Chamberlayne, an old family friend

(Opposite) Hashim and Azam Khan – the two great brothers who dominated the squash world in the 1950s

(Below) Two men who figured prominently in Barrington's early career – SRA secretary John Horry, on the left, with the Egyptian Abou Taleb, who won the British Open three times

The men behind the miracle. Azam Khan (left) and Nasrullah Khan sharing Jonah's triumph after he had beaten Australian Dick Carter in the 1966-67 British Amateur Championship and achieved the double of the Open and Amateur Championships in the same season

(Opposite) Barrington steps in to volley against Aftab Jawaid of Pakistan in the final of the 1970 British Open at Edgbaston Priory which he won 9-1, 9-2, 9-6

Jonah attacks from the front during his quarter-final victory over Australian Ken Hiscoe before a packed gallery at Abbeydale in the 1972-73 British Open

(Opposite) Jonah drops his racket in exhaustion after winning the marathon 2 hours 13 minutes British Open final at Edgbaston Priory Club in December 1969, with a dejected Geoff Hunt in the background. 'I've never seen two sportsmen so exhausted,' said the photographer Ken Kelly

(Below) Seven famous winners of the British Open pictured outside Pakistan International Airlines squash complex in Karachi in 1976. From left to right, Azam Khan (four opens), Geoff Hunt (eight), Hashim Khan (seven), Jonah Barrington (six), Roshan Khan (one), Mohibullah Khan Senior (one) and Qamar Zaman (one)

What could they find to smile about after 2 hours 13 minutes on court?
Jonah and Geoff Hunt after their epic 1969 British Open at Edgaston Priory

(Opposite) A text-book backhand dropshot from Jonah demands Hunt's
concentration

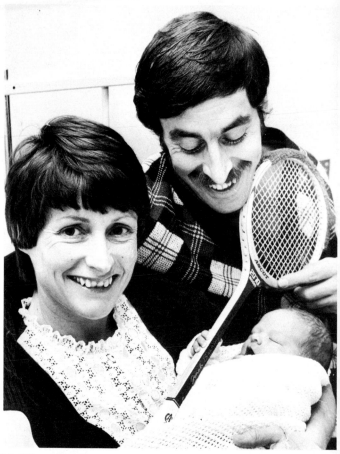

Madeline and Jonah shortly after the birth of their first child,
Nicholas Barrington, in February 1975

(Above right) Egypt's Ali Aziz demonstrates the unorthodox methods the
game's top players employ to keep the ball in play. You won't see a
forehand like this in the coaching manual, but then Ali has never read it

(Below right) A traffic jam on the T as Jonah follows through against the
mercurial Qamar Zaman in the 1980 Northampton Masters at Wembley

Jonah plays a drop shot against Ahmed Safwat in the third round of the 1978 British Open at Wembley. 'Artful Ahmed' appears to have it covered but he lost the match 7-9, 9-3, 8-10, 9-4, 0-9

(Opposite) Maximum effort by Jonah in the 1975 *Superstars* gym tests before he walked out of the competition

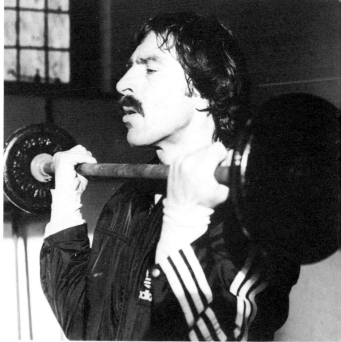

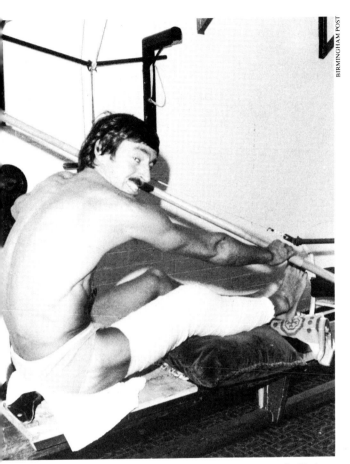

No matter how incapacitated, Jonah will always find a way to train. He is pictured here on a canoe ergometer which he used to maintain his fitness while recovering from a knee operation in 1981

(Above left) Leading players from the world of squash gathered for a World Doubles tournament. From left to right, Geoff Hunt, Hiddy Jahan, Mo Asran, Ken Hiscoe, Abou Taleb, Jonah Barrington, Gogi Alauddin and, partially in the photograph on the far right, Mike Corby

(Below left) A study in concentration as Jonah weight-trains in the gymnasium of his Solihull home in 1981

reaching for his running shoes, and it cannot be without coincidence that the last three world champions of any substance, Barrington, Hunt and Jahangir Khan, have all adhered to training schedules dramatically cruel both in intensity and content. Jonah's training schedule is detailed elsewhere in this book but Hunt's regime when building up for a major championship was no less startling and could only ever be undertaken by a man who recognised that, for the endurance athlete, pain has to be experienced on a daily basis so that the element of fear is removed from the condition.

'Hunt,' says Jonah, 'would alternate hard, steady running at about six-and-a-half minute mile pace with intervals, basically quarter- and half-miles. Initially his steady runs would be four or five miles and he would do perhaps seven quarters at 75-second pace with a 45-second recovery. He would progress until he would be running ten miles continuously and as many as thirty interval quarter miles. Later in the day he would put in a two-hour stint on court, playing and practising. Len Steward, the Australian international, has told me just how tired Geoff was in those court sessions. Len was a regular sparring partner and always marvelled at Geoff's will to win in spite of being on his knees from his morning's running. To Geoff and myself every game was terribly important and the commitment to win every one, even a practice game, was never in doubt. I believe in his final training effort in the Australian summer of 1981, Geoff pushed his body beyond the limits of endurance and, regrettably, the inevitable end must have been hastened.'

Hunt admits it was defeats by Jonah, and particularly losing the Australian Open to him in 1970, that made him commit himself fully to intensive training. But he has no doubt that Barrington was the fittest player he ever encountered: 'On a cold court, I could sometimes get on top of him and beat him convincingly in less than an hour. My game was based on attack and pressure and the colder conditions suited my game as it was easier to put the ball away. But at other times, usually in the hotter conditions when Jonah had decided to stay on court and extend the game by lobbing to the back, I knew I was going to feel the pinch. There were many matches like that. When he really extended a match, he would win the majority of them. Unfortunately for me, this would normally happen in the final of a major tournament, played on a hotter court. When Jonah was in this mood he was very hard to beat. And in the early days, when I found myself in one of these marathons, I knew I was really going to be in trouble the next day.'

Most of their championship matches were marvellously similar in that they were usually long five-setters in which Hunt would threaten to roll Barrington off the court through his speed of play and all-round brilliance. Barrington would ride out the storm by endeavouring to play the ball tighter and deeper and doing everything he could to prevent Hunt from setting up one of his lethal volleying attacks. He would throw in the occasional drop shot, usually on the backhand, to remind Hunt that his thought process was still functioning and wait for the sign that he had begun to draw out Hunt's sting. But he would have to be infinitely patient and accurate for extraordinary periods of time as Hunt was capable of volleying like an automaton.

However, experience taught Barrington that if he could keep Hunt on court for long enough – an hour-and-a-half, say – there was a possibility that he would get cramp. Jonah enjoyed an enormous physical and psychological ascendancy over the majority of his opponents but the only doubt he had been able to instil into Hunt's mind concerned the length of the match. The three best examples of Jonah's battle-plan are the 1969 British Open at Edgbaston Priory in Birmingham, the 1970 Australian Open in Melbourne and the 1972 British Open at Abbeydale, Sheffield.

After the 1969 Open final, which lasted for hours and 13 minutes (then a world record), both men were completely spent, to such an extent that the normally loquacious Barrington was for once lost for words. 'Neither of us could muster much enthusiasm for an interview. I said nothing, he said nothing, I had won, he had lost. I don't think I was as physically tired as Geoffrey but mentally I was just as shattered. This was because Nasrullah had told me that under no circumstances was I to play a single ball short from behind Hunt. Throughout the whole match, I was not to play a drop or boast from behind or level with him and I maintained that for the whole of the match. It was terribly difficult but with Geoff's speed of movement and weight of shot, if I had played short from behind him and not been accurate, I would only have been playing myself into trouble.

'What I remember about all my long matches with Geoff is that afterwards I would generally not feel like playing him again for three months. I had done my marathon, I had stretched myself to the limit and I would be totally unable to make another effort against him. Geoff's athleticism, however, was so great that he could recover his physical resources and slot back into his normal game straightaway; that was one of the advantages of his youth compared to me.'

Hunt's recuperative powers were indeed phenomenal but they seemed to let him down after the 1969 British Open. 'I suffered from cramp in that match,' says the Australian. 'I was very distressed afterwards and couldn't eat or drink properly until the following day. The main symptoms were a feeling of having a great pocket of air trapped inside my stomach and I was unable to keep anything down. It was the hardest game I ever played and I remember that, after it, I couldn't sleep at all. I was certainly in a worse state than Jonah.'

A typical Hunt–Barrington drama was played out in Albert Park, Melbourne, in the final of the 1970 Australian Open, although for Geoff, playing in front of his home crowd, it was to be a tragedy in five sets. For these two marathon runners, the match was something of a sprint, lasting 95 minutes, but it was certainly not without its dramatic moments. Having been 2–1 down, as he had been at Edgbaston Priory, Jonah clawed his way back into the match and was so exhausted by his efforts that he had to be helped off the court by Abou Taleb. By 1970, Taleb was a pretty solid citizen but, as the many photographs taken after the match reveal, he was struggling to support the weight of Jonah who was obviously quite unable to coordinate any part of his frame. And what of the loser? Apart from cramp again (making one wonder just how many titles he would have won had Jonah cured the condition earlier), Hunt says that early on in the match, Jonah hit him with his racket and cut his eye and a lot of people have always asked him why he didn't have it attended to. His shirt was covered in blood and it looked quite dramatic but 'the thing was that if I had stopped to have it attended to, I'd never have got going again. The blood wasn't getting in my eye so it didn't affect me in any way. Jonah knew that if I stopped to have it fixed, I might never get going again so, in a great show of concern, he rushed around saying he wanted to fix it himself!'

In 1972 the two champions played another great match for the British Open title at Abbeydale. Although neither could have been aware of it at the time, it was to be the last occasion on which they were to meet in competition for the game's major title. The following year, surprisingly, Hunt was removed from the Open by Gogi Alauddin, who was then beaten in the final by Jonah, the last time Jonah was to win the title.

The 1972 Open final stuck rigidly to the script of earlier Barrington–Hunt confrontations – if you have something the public likes, why bother to change it? Barrington's health during his preparation for the championship had been poor, for apart from all the usual aches and pains which are the lot of the endurance athlete in constant training, he had spent most of December in agony with compacted wisdom teeth. By the time the final arrived, Barrington wasn't feeling at all well and he didn't manage to score a point for about 25 minutes. But he was determined to hang on and eventually Hunt cracked.

In the second game, with Jonah still seeking his first point and fighting the diarrhoea which had been troubling him for some days, Hunt hit a cracking boast to Jonah's forehand, stretching him to the limit. But Jonah managed to throw up a beautiful lob down the side wall that was descending to a perfect length when it hit a woman spectator leaning over the sidewall gallery on the head! Fully aware of Jonah's fiery temperament, the crowd held its breath. But instead of the anticipated eruption, Jonah addressed the spectator very politely. 'Lovey,' he said, 'don't you think I've got enough problems down here without you putting your head in the way?' Hunt, who had seen his opponent erupt in enraged fashion all over the world with far less provocation, was so amazed by this untypical reaction that he lost concentration for the first time and allowed Jonah into the match.

Nicholas Barrington was also at Abbeydale in 1972 and the spectacle he witnessed was gruesome: 'At the end of the fourth set, I went down behind the tin where there was a glass viewing panel. Halfway through the fifth, I couldn't watch any more because Geoff had turned a sickening colour and the expression of pain on his face was awful – I thought he was going to die.' Analogies of boxers teetering dazed and confused along the ropes readily spring to mind, but it was quite clear that Hunt was suffering another serious attack of cramp. 'At the end of the fourth, I could feel my wrist seizing up,' he recalls. 'So I decided to go for the doctor.' (For those not acquainted with Australianese, this means that Hunt threw caution aside for one final violent assault.) 'I threw everything at him and got to about 7–0 before the cramp got to the rest of my body and Jonah went through me.'

Having endured all those mind-bending hours on court with Hunt, Jonah is uniquely qualified to assess the man whom the record books say was the greatest player in the game's history:

> He was without doubt the most gracefully balanced mover we have ever seen in squash and, in my mind's eye, I can always see that characteristic forward lean as he flowed around the court. He was certainly among the fastest movers of the day, although many say that Hashim Khan was even faster. But Geoff was not only a fast mover, he played at such a fast pace too, especially during his early phase.
>
> When I first saw him in 1964, his reflex work around the centre of the court was extraordinary – in a class of its own. But later, he became a completely

different player with a much more cautious, calculating game. That was how he got on top of Zaman.

Hunt wasn't averse to a bit of psychological warfare either. On court, he would sometimes try to psyche me out. He'd talk to me, always through clenched teeth so nobody knew what was going on. If I hit the tin or made a tactical error on a pressure point, he'd say: 'Cost you the game, cost you the game.'

Geoff was the ultimate competitor. He would never give in. If he was beaten, he would go away and work harder. There was always an aura of calmness about him. He was certain that whatever he planned would always work out. In a quiet way he would make it obvious that he could solve any problems, such as those he had to face against Zaman in the last phases of his career. But throughout that period he always gave the impression that he could win the big one. His mind was phenomenal. If there was ever an element of doubt, he never allowed anyone to see it.

Throughout every training session during my days as Open Champion, I would be thinking about my next confrontation with Hunt, and even if it was six months ahead, I would always use it as my motivation. When I was playing my best, I felt he was the only player against whom I was at a considerable disadvantage. I could flow against the majority of the other players but never against him. I did have a problem with the great strokeplayer Hiscoe despite the fact that I felt I was a better player overall. But against Hunt, I knew he was on a higher athletic plane and that I was going to have to put in another grinding performance.

When their rivalry was at its peak, many of the so-called experts, usually of the beer-swilling persuasion, were critical of Jonah for using what they saw as negative tactics against Hunt . . . driving and lobbing remorselessly to a length for hour after hour. Unable to appreciate the mind-warping discipline required to adhere to these tactics for interminable periods of time, they were all too quick to write off Jonah as being a mere retriever. Such unintelligent comments only add fuel to Jonah's belief that the vast majority of spectators of top-class sport fail to understand what they see. Furthermore, such criticism of Jonah's play and tactics has always amazed the man best qualified to judge – Geoff Hunt. 'There is a terrific misunderstanding about length,' says Hunt. 'For it is not just length as such, one uses length to force the opening position. It is as an attacking as well as a defensive ploy. Jonah had the ability to keep himself out of trouble, while ensuring I was always in difficulties, by controlling the ball to a good length. He always had me a yard further back on the court than anyone else and this made him very difficult to play, it made it hard for me to get the front position. In my opinion, Jonah won all his matches this way. Achieving a good length is the basis of the game and no one will ever become a good player until they learn this lesson. Jonah was absolutely brilliant at it.'

In Hunt's opinion Barrington, apart from his remarkable fitness and marvellous control of length, possessed other qualities which made him an outstanding player: 'What I most liked about Jonah was his competitiveness. He would try as hard as he could – when he was really out to win he would never give in. His biggest asset, though, was his squash brain. He always considered where he wanted to put the ball and where it would do the most damage.'

Despite the admiration the two men clearly have for each other, there are a number of matters that still rankle between them, little wounds and suspicions that will never entirely heal. Primarily, Jonah smarts at what he considers to have been the underhand conspiracy and secrecy which cloaked both Hunt's and Hiscoe's decision to turn professional in 1971. It was quite clear that they had no apparent intention of including him in their plans, despite the fact that he had been trying, for some time, to persuade them to join him as a professional. When they announced their decision, it came as a total surprise to Jonah, especially as they had also set up their own promotional activities without considering him.

At that stage, I felt that my mental resources were already beginning to dwindle. Although I was physically fine, I was finding it very difficult to gear myself in the way that I wanted because I had put so much effort into my game for so many years. It was as if I had conquered Everest again and again but sensed I didn't have sufficient stimulus to make another ascent. But the way in which they rejected me was just what I needed to motivate myself. In a way they did me a favour, and when Kenny told the press that the only reason they had ever lost to me in the past was that I had been a full-time professional while they had only been part-time amateurs, I was furious. That one remark provided me with a lasting springboard for the next few years. I resented their actions terribly because, while I had a fundamental respect for them as players, I sensed that they wanted to see me fouled up. During their first tour over here, Hiscoe would never let me go anywhere near Geoff in case I wanted to talk about any plans that I had. Kenny kept Geoff very much under his wing and he did not want me in on the act.

The following year, Jonah went to Australia to play in the Vigorade promotion with Hunt, Hiscoe and Gogi Alauddin, who by that time had also taken the plunge and turned professional. But according to Jonah, there was no team spirit, it was a case of them against him: 'I couldn't understand why we didn't all get together to discuss how to set up some four-man promotions to make some money. They just got on and did their own thing. I was right out of it and they didn't hide the fact. At that time there were two camps, the Australians and me. Taleb and Jawaid had gone and I was all that was standing in their way. I would say I have always been susceptible to paranoia – I can recognise this – but when I think back, I can remember how consumed with rage I was that they were determined to exclude me from their plans. There wasn't a five-minute conversation when we would have sat down and discussed what we professionals were going to do for each other.'

110

Hiscoe, now a successful squash club proprietor in Sydney, is very much aware that they failed to capitalise on the famous Hunt–Barrington rivalry: 'With hindsight, I now realise it would have been better for all of us, and better for the game, if we had included Jonah in our plans. I suppose we lost sight of the commercial possibilities because, as Australians, the most important priority is always to beat the British. But you must remember how green we were at the time, and there is no doubt we were very suspicious of him.'

Rex Bellamy, however, understood the underlying reasons: 'Because the Australians are known as gamblers, we tend to forget just how conservative a people they are. Hiscoe and Hunt were very reluctant about the whole deal. Being the great Australians they are, they tended to be suspicious of this glib, fast-talking Englishman who seemed to have the answers to everything and was never slow to give people the benefit of his opinions.'

But Geoff remains deeply aware of the impact Jonah has had on the game and his role in expanding it, especially in Britain, and also of the work he has done in enhancing the status of the professional.

When Jonah turned professional, the coaching professional in Britain was very much a second-class citizen, and definitely an employee. Not only did he have to teach the club members, he also had to pick up the ball for them between rallies. Jonah completely reversed that situation until the professional came to be regarded as the top expert in his field and a figure to be respected.

At times, he is very generous. He thinks a lot of the pros and he's done a lot of work for them. But there have been many occasions on which he has withdrawn from tournaments 'because of injury', when it is clearly apparent that there's not much wrong with him. His level of on-court competitiveness has created aggro with other players who consider that he has always selected his tournaments carefully, to deny them the chance to have a crack at him. I don't think they would have beaten him anyway, but everyone likes to have a shot at the top man.

In my opinion he has a split personality. He can often be very bubbly and talkative; his enthusiasm becomes contagious. He can keep a group of people entertained for hours. But on the other hand, he can be brusque to the point of rudeness, and walk straight past you as if he doesn't know you. He tends not to socialise. If he loses, he doesn't want to see anyone. If he wins, he wants to get away to prepare for the next day.

Jonah, in turn, is not entirely uncritical of Hunt, his main point being that he could have done so much more to promote the game: 'Geoff has never really enthused about squash, he has never sold his personality – and he has a lot more personality than people think. He is certainly not the iceberg people imagine.' Jonah also suspects that Hunt was jealous of his knack of being able to command the headlines long after his days as an effective force at the ultimate level were over. But he will also admit that he was envious of Hunt's success on court and the publicity it generated when his own time was past.

However, even though a few minor niggles and jealousies persist, the walls of Jonah's study are still hung with many photographs of Geoff Hunt in action. Looking at them, he admits that he can never fail to admire the athleticism of the man to whose defeat he devoted such a large part of his life. But those same photographs must surely also serve to re-mind Jonah Barrington just how good a player he himself must have been to have beaten Geoff Hunt in all those epic finals.

8. *Madeline*

She has never forgotten seeing him for the first time. He was standing in the hallway of Mike Grundy's Sheffield home making a telephone call, his bare feet clearly visible beneath an old grey tracksuit. Those feet may have been just about the ugliest she had ever seen, but God, she thought, what a good-looking man. Madeline Ibbotson had often seen Jonah Barrington's name in newspapers but this was the first time they had ever met.

Barrington's attempt to win the British Open for the third consecutive time had come to an abrupt halt at Abbeydale in January 1969. Not for the first time, Cam Nancarrow had put paid to his aspirations in a major tournament, and the kind of championship he specialised in winning at that. The Australian had defeated him in the semi-finals, in straight games, 9–4, 9–5, 10–8, plunging the Cornishman into yet another of his black depressions. Nothing would convince Barrington that he had deserved to lose that match – he had undoubtedly played the better squash and, in his view, the referee's amazing tolerance of Nancarrow's blocking tactics had cost him victory. No doubt others would have made some attempt to relax and enjoy themselves after such a defeat and forgotten about today until tomorrow. But defeat for Barrington inevitably meant more punishment. It was as if he always had to prove, both to the world and himself, that such adversity merely engendered in him yet greater resolve and instant retribution in the form of even more gruelling training.

And so it was that, immediately after his untimely dismissal from the Open, Jonah, then staying with Mike Grundy, the Yorkshire County player, telephoned Derek Ibbotson, the former world mile record-holder, with a request that they train together. The following day, Jonah was out early running with the Ibbotsons in Sheffield's Graves Park.

Madeline Ibbotson, a former British 800-metres indoor record-holder, who at the age of eighteen was the youngest woman in the world to run a mile in under five minutes, still remembers that run:

> Derek was showing off a bit and the run was really quite hard. Jonah had only lost the night before and, knowing him as I now do, he must have been terribly drained. But he kept up with us all the time. I think he was a bit concerned at first though because, from the start, I was doing my usual heavy breathing. There were some terrific hills and we really lashed around. I could see him glancing at me, occasionally thinking 'Blimey, she's not going to last very long', but after six miles I was still there, doing my heavy breathing. I'm sure he thought it was very dramatic.
>
> After we'd finished, we started hopping to strengthen the legs. Now, poor old Jonah had eaten a late curry the night before and had obviously found the run a bit hard. He never said anything though, but, with all the hopping, he had to disappear into the loo for about ten minutes. Then he was back hopping again. I was impressed. I hadn't expected a squash player to run so well but that session certainly proved just how fit he was. Derek and I often used to meet Lyn Davies, Mary Rand and other athletes at Ron Pickering's house at weekends and although they were specialist athletes, they couldn't run distance the way Jonah could. I was among the leading British women's 800-metres runners and could get up quite a pace. But here was a squash player who could run six or eight miles and keep up with us. It takes a lot of training and running to achieve that.

The following morning, Barrington was out training with the Ibbotsons again and after lunch took them both round to the Sheffield club to meet Geraldine and Nasrullah Khan. Madeline immediately sensed that the pair were

114

wary of her. 'They weren't particularly gracious to Derek either,' she recalls. 'I realised that they were very possessive of Jonah and seemed to resent us helping him train. We just weren't part of the family.'

Nevertheless, Jonah was enjoying his training sessions with the Ibbotsons, and when they invited him to stay on for a couple of days, he accepted readily. Before long, he was visiting them regularly at weekends and once the gruelling training was done, Derek Ibbotson tried valiantly to encourage the Monk of the West End to stray into the realms of normality.

Derek's first move was to find a girlfriend for Jonah if he went out in the evening, and that was a basic mistake. It just wasn't Jonah's style . . . he didn't want it, he didn't like it and in the end he said so. But Derek was only trying to relax the guy. For three whole years, under Naz's strict control, he'd worked flat out, being told no drink, no women, no one-night stands. He was utterly dedicated to his training, so much so that he'd forgotten how to relax.

At the end of the day, he'd sit huddled in a chair like a little old man. He loved to talk but every aspect of his conversation revolved around training and squash. As far as he was concerned, there was nothing else. He told us how he was determined to go on forever, but we knew it wasn't possible. We tried to explain that even as athletes we'd get sozzled on a Saturday night and then pay for it on Sunday, running ourselves into the ground. Even in my early years, I'd have a few lagers at the end of a meeting to unwind, but Jonah wasn't interested. He didn't go to parties; he didn't go anywhere; he didn't have anything or anybody.

All that time my liking for Jonah was growing enormously. There was a kind of aura about him. He had the most endearing charm and he wasn't at all conceited, but the one thing that never ceased to amaze me was his simplicity . . . he was so clear-thinking, so sound, he could work anything out. He was certainly very good-looking too. A slight man with clear brown eyes and the semblance of a tan: I thought he looked more Spanish than English. I was aware that I was physically attracted to him and knew how much I liked him but, at that time, I hadn't the slightest intention of getting involved with him. After all, I was a married woman with three daughters.

Both Derek and Madeline suspected that Jonah's obsession with his sport could lead to his downfall, especially as time began to take its toll. 'We both felt that if he didn't find something else at the end of the line, he would break down.' It was not long before the irony of Madeline's words was to become clear.

The following winter Jonah was still training occasionally with the Ibbotsons and preparing hard for his forthcoming fifteen-match series with Geoff Hunt. In the event, his Abbeydale encounter in the series with the young Australian was not a total success but, true to form, he continued to drive himself relentlessly towards even higher peaks of fitness.

In the summer of 1970, Barrington found himself in Durham, visiting businessman Brian Hewitt, whose company manufactured squash equipment. Aware that his journey south would take him close to the Ibbotsons' home in Huddersfield, he decided to see if he could fit in another training session. Madeline answered the 'phone and explained that Derek, a sales representative with Puma, the sports equipment manufacturers, was away in Mexico, for the World Cup, but nevertheless Jonah was most welcome to come and stay anyway. And so the next day Jonah was in Huddersfield, together with two other guests of Madeline, pole-vaulter Geoff Elliott and the wife of Derek's German counterpart, who was also in Mexico. Madeline was certain that her husband wouldn't object to the invitation she had extended to the squash player who was by now, after all, a family friend. 'But when he rang, I was surprised to realise just how excited I was that he was coming; it would be the first time that we had been alone together. We hadn't seen each other for a number of months but the moment I opened the door I saw that he was wearing a gold ring. I felt rather deflated somehow; I thought he had got engaged.'

Although Jonah had originally intended to stay a couple of days at the most, time passed quickly and he seemed settled, both with his training routine and the domestic background of the Ibbotson house:

One evening, we were all sitting around drinking wine, and even Jonah, to my great surprise, had managed to put a few glasses away. Perhaps he was beginning to feel a bit sorry for himself but he tried to explain how, for the first time, he was finding his life as a squash player incomplete. He had nothing to fall back on and was always lonely, especially when he was away. He didn't know how to cope with himself. We all listened and talked for a while but when the others had gone to bed I told him about Derek and me and how utterly depressed I had become when I was told by friends that he had been having affairs when he was away. After all, we had been married for fourteen years. I can't say I was jealous but I did think I had failed somehow. In the end, I was so depressed about the whole thing that I had an affair or two myself. I suppose I needed to boost my morale. And apart from all this, Derek had now been away in Mexico for four weeks and I hadn't heard a single thing from him. Not a 'phone call, not even so much as a postcard. Nothing.

Jonah was absolutely shocked when he heard all this. He'd always been certain that we'd had a 100 per cent marriage and had never tried to get involved. But from there on, it was the start of things between us. I remember telling him at the time that I needed an affair and he needed an affair and that was that. As far as I was concerned, there was no other future.

By the time Derek did eventually contact me, Jonah and I had been together for two weeks and were virtually inseparable. The morning I was going to collect Derek from the airport, Jonah insisted that he was going to stay and have it all out. But I made him pack his things and go because the last thing I wanted was an ugly confrontation. As far as I was concerned, my marriage had been a problem for some years but now at last I was clear about what I was going to do. I was going to leave Derek, but I would do it in my own way and in my own time.

When I saw Derek at the airport, coming through customs, it made me all the more determined to tell him everything and tell him straight. I explained calmly that our marriage was no longer worthwhile. I told him all about Jonah and could see that he was shocked and angry. From then on he refused to discuss the matter at all. He saw no reason at all why we should break up our marriage and told me never to see Jonah again. I must say I was amazed at how jealous he was as I didn't believe at that stage that he could have any real affection for me anyway.

For his part, Barrington had always regarded Derek Ibbotson as a happy family man with a secure home and a wife who could not only understand his sporting life but also be involved in it. 'I had not the slightest suspicion that their marriage was in difficulties. I was just maintaining the same daily routine I had continued for six years although I was increasingly conscious that I was getting older. I was nearly thirty and I suppose I was getting a bit depressed about the future. Of course, I had always been attracted to Madeline, but I would never really admit it to anyone, not even myself, until it appeared that their marriage was beyond repair.'

In January 1971, Madeline left Derek Ibbotson for Jonah Barrington. She had purposely given herself time to reflect on her initial decision and was still certain where her future lay. Leaving behind Huddersfield and the family to which she was devoted, she travelled down to London, where she was to meet Jonah at the Lansdowne Club. But by an unfortunate turn of fate, the first person she ran into was the *Daily Mail* sportswriter Terry O'Connor, who had known the Ibbotsons for many years. What was Madeline doing at the Lansdowne? How was Derek? She had come to watch some squash, she told him as calmly as she could, but O'Connor, his journalist's instinct telling him that this explanation lacked conviction, called Derek. And within twenty-four hours, the full story was to be in the *Daily Mail*.

Even allowing for the fact that Barrington was not altogether unused to handling a crisis, either on or off the court, he knew that the consequences of O'Connor's story could prove intensely difficult, both for him and Madeline. Turning to his good friend Mike Corby, he telephoned him for advice: 'I've got a problem. Madeline. Derek knows everything; he's divorcing her and she's going to divorce him. It's going to be all over the bloody papers tomorrow. I don't know what to do.' Somewhat unhelpfully, so Jonah thought at the time, Corby burst out laughing: 'Well, big fish. You *have* got a problem. Look, you can do one of two things – marry her or get on your bike. And my advice is to get on your bike and pedal like hell.' Madeline was somewhat bewildered to find Mike Corby giving her the same advice too. She'd be a fool to get involved with Jonah. But wasn't Corby Jonah's best friend? Yes, he was, and that was exactly why he was giving her that advice too.

So, there seemed to be nothing left save hope that other more important stories laid claim to the *Mail*'s pages and that what was after all a purely private matter would not be laid out for all and sundry to gape and gossip. But it was not to be. IBBOTSON'S WIFE SAYS: I LOVE SQUASH STAR was the rather dramatic headline in the *Daily Mail* on 14 January 1971. There was also a picture of Madeline getting into her car outside the Lansdowne together with photographs of Derek and Jonah. Terry O'Connor's story read:

The wife of Derek Ibbotson, former world mile record-holder, has left him because of her love for Jonah Barrington, world No 1 squash player.

Ibbotson said last night in Huddersfield, Yorkshire, where he lives with his three daughters in a £10,000 five-bedroom house: 'Madeline has left me and the family.'

Mrs Ibbotson told me: 'I have left Derek because I love Jonah. It's heartbreaking to leave the children, but it is better they stay together, and Derek is a very good father.'

Ibbotson and Barrington were great friends and trained together. They met in February 1969 when Barrington sought Ibbotson's advice on how to improve his fitness.

Madeline Ibbotson was an international middle-distance runner when she met her husband. They have been married for 15 years and have three daughters, Christine, 13, Nicola, 10 and Georgina, 3.

Mrs Ibbotson is 35, seven years older than Barrington. She left home last Thursday.

On Monday, she accompanied Barrington to the Lansdowne Club in London for the British Amateur Squash Championships. She lunched with him at the club on Tuesday and then drove him to Cheltenham for a tournament that night.

Ibbotson won a bronze medal in the Melbourne Olympic Games in 1957 and broke the world mile record in 1957.

He now coaches athletes and the Manchester City football team, apart from occasionally running as a professional.

He said last night: 'Barrington stayed at my home about once a month to relax away from London and we trained together.'

Before the break came the Ibbotsons tried to settle their differences.

Ibbotson, 38, said: 'Recently Madeline decided to put the family first. I still hope she might think the matter over again.'

Last night Barrington was at St Annes-on-Sea, Lancashire, where he is the No 1 seed in this week's North-West Open Squash Championship.

He said: 'I don't wish to say anything.'

During Barrington's build-up to squash dominance he lived the life of a monk. He once told me: 'I have been teetotal now for five years, and I gave up all association with women for 22 months. Even now I return to a monastic life of celibacy months before a national championship.'

The story rebounded, not only around the sporting world but everywhere else, too. Within an hour or two, telephones were ringing all over the country, with newspaper men following up every angle they could think of.

Geraldine, taken aback at all the fuss, was most concerned that her younger brother was getting himself involved with a married woman who had three children. But down in Cornwall, Nicholas Barrington retained a sense of humour. 'There's no such thing as bad publicity,' he told Geraldine. 'There's only one thing worse than being talked about and that's not being talked about. Just make sure they all mention that his brother's a solicitor in Falmouth and he's short of clients.'

Aside from the reactions of Geraldine and Nick, Jonah had no doubt that if his father had still been alive, he would have disapproved strongly of what he was doing. Apart from anything else, Madeline was a Catholic and Major Barrington had never been over-fond of Catholics. But when Jonah took Madeline down to Marratons, his mother was much more concerned that three children were involved. It was not long however before she took her younger son on one side and whispered urgently, 'What would your father have said? She's a Papist!' But as time went by, Mrs Barrington warmed to her considerably and a couple of years later, during the last six months of Mrs Barrington's life, Madeline was one of those who nursed her with such loyalty and devotion as she died a slow and painful death from cancer.

After the story had broken in the *Daily Mail*, the outspoken squash star and the wife of the famous British athlete were pursued with some intensity by the newspapers. For a month, the couple stayed at the St Anne's home of Clive Francis, while Jonah toured with the northern professional, and the newshounds even set up camp outside the house.

Cam Nancarrow, who was also a guest at the Francis home, recalls: 'We were all out in the bush somewhere in

Lancashire and there were more reporters outside the house than I'd ever seen in my life. You'd have thought Jonah was all four Beatles rolled into one. It was a bit of a problem getting Jonah out of the house. One morning Clive sauntered out of the front door quite casually; I'm sure the press guys thought he was going to paint the fence or something. Then, at a pre-arranged signal, we rushed Jonah out of the house and into the back of the car with a blanket over his head. Before the door was even shut we got going bloody quickly and managed to lose them.'

Both Jonah and Madeline were totally shocked by the attitude of the press: 'The *Daily Mail* must have made up their quotes,' says Jonah, 'because neither of us would say anything about our affair – and never have. It was a private matter: we didn't even give them a "No comment." But they were certainly hot on the story and just seemed to materialise everywhere. They were even clambering around the bedroom window, and it seemed to be ages before they got sick of chasing us around.'

All in all, it was a very emotional time. Apart from the almost intolerable persistence of the press, Madeline was missing her children terribly and everywhere she went she was regarded disdainfully as the scarlet woman. She recalls that by the end of that month at the Francis home, they were both dangerously near to a nervous breakdown. 'We were under so much stress. The press were absolutely determined to get a quote out of us but we were just as determined to talk to no one. I couldn't understand why we were attracting so much attention. I had always been a respectable married woman and even though I was having an affair, I certainly wasn't trying to be brazen about it. We just wanted to be together but privacy was out of the question.'

For Barrington himself, the situation presented a terrible dilemma. He was in no doubt whatsoever about his feelings for Madeline but what would happen if Derek Ibbotson wasn't given custody of the three girls? Could he seriously consider taking them on and would his attitude to Madeline change in the knowledge that he had broken up a family? Madeline, too, was naturally concerned about her children and desperately unhappy at being away from the three girls who had always meant so much to her and always will. If she and Jonah ever happened to be driving past a school while the children were streaming out of the gates on their way home, her thoughts became too painful for her to bear and she would break down, the tears streaming uncontrollably down her cheeks. Therefore, it was hardly to be wondered at that when Jonah went off to Canada to play squash, Madeline decided to return home.

But while Jonah was in Canada, he had the opportunity to consider his position carefully and without the extreme pressures to which they had both been subjected. It was painfully clear to him that he had made the most dreadful mistake – he should never have allowed her to go back to Derek and he telephoned her to say so. 'It had obviously hit Jonah's system badly: he wanted to find a proper home and was only too willing to have the girls with us. He hadn't been able to play squash and had never felt so utterly dejected in his life. I listened to him carefully and knew that I wanted to return to him. But I would have to take my time as I wanted to plan things in the most decent way.'

For Jonah, however, life without Madeline was hard to bear. In the summer of 1971 he was training the British team for the World Amateur Championships. 'I was totally miserable and missed her more than I could ever believe possible. It was very difficult to concentrate on the job in hand and I knew I wanted her with me.'

He did not have long to wait before Madeline's role in the Ibbotson household came to an abrupt conclusion when her husband returned one evening from a Manchester City game. 'He'd obviously had a lot to drink and was in a filthy temper. We had the most violent row. Nothing like it had ever happened before and I fled out of the house and went to stay with friends. I never went back to him again.'

Within a matter of weeks, Jonah and Madeline were reunited and set about making plans for the future. Jonah disliked the idea of living in London and consequently when the West Warwickshire Squash Club near Birmingham offered him free training facilities – the first club ever to do so – they moved to the Midlands and set up home in

Solihull in a small flat kindly provided by Peter Webb, a club member and a dedicated squash enthusiast.

The flat, over one of Peter Webb's hairdressing salons, was the first real home for Jonah and Madeline. The next step was to obtain Madeline's divorce and get married. Derek Ibbotson, however, was in no mood to make things easy and as innumerable letters were dispatched from solicitor to solicitor Jonah realised it could be a protracted process: 'Initially, Derek was only prepared to give Madeline a divorce provided it was one-sided, citing me. But the moment she cross-petitioned and he realised that all his peccadillos were going to be aired, he suddenly agreed that he would not contest matters. And so there was no case in the end, though he was awarded custody of the children.'

But before the divorce was final there was to be yet another chapter to complicate matters. Madeline had been looking forward to life with Jonah in their little flat above the hairdressing shop and was busying herself in creating a home for them both when Nasrullah Khan's eldest son Aman came to spend a few weeks with them – and stayed six months! 'Naz had the same attitude to his sons that he had always had to Jonah. He used to bully and drive them unmercifully and Aman was getting very fed up. So Jonah, who can be as soft as putty, invited him to stay with us. Now we had only just got together again and things were still pretty stormy at that stage. Jonah was finding it difficult to adapt and so was I, totally cut off from my children. All of a sudden there we were with our own resident chaperone; it was hardly ideal. There was no real home to look after so I decided that I'd better train with them twice a day. I ferried them everywhere in the car and when they were on court, I was left sitting around like a lemon. After six months I'd had enough. For heaven's sake, here I was nursemaiding two grown men while I was the mother of three children from whom I was totally cut off. So I left Jonah for the second time, but as soon as he realised it had indeed been an impractical way of living, I came back.'

Monday 2 July, 1973, was a bright summer's day and Jonah and Madeline were duly married at Solihull Registry Office. It was a quiet yet none the less sincere ceremony with only a handful of people present, including Peter Webb, who acted as best man, and a few members of the West Warwicks Squash Club.

Madeline Barrington was fully aware that her new husband was a rather disorganised man in certain ways. For example, sartorial matters had never been a priority, she had never been in any doubt about that: 'I found a pair of grey trousers stuck over the back of a chair in the bedroom one day. They were a bit ragged so I put them in the washing machine, but before they had been in there a couple of minutes, Jonah came padding into the kitchen in his track suit demanding to know what I'd done with his trousers as they were the only pair he had. When I pointed to them whirling around in the washing machine he was livid, and as I couldn't stop laughing it made him worse. I still can't get him to go out and buy anything.'

Despite his success, Jonah only had about £200 in his bank account on the day they were married. Always generous with his hard-earned money, he never seemed to be concerned about his financial welfare. Madeline regularly found unbanked cheques in his pockets, some of them for substantial sums.

To the world at large, Jonah Barrington may be the famous squash player who walked off with his training partner's wife. The fact that that training partner was a famous athlete who had captured the imagination of the British public only served to make matters worse as did the existence of three young girls who had been left with a broken home. But what the public were totally unaware of was that Jonah had only become involved with Madeline after the breakdown of her marriage. Jonah has always maintained a great admiration for Derek Ibbotson as an athlete and is quick to confirm that there is no way he would have allowed himself to become involved with Madeline before being certain that their marriage was over: 'Derek was a very popular figure and so it was natural for me to be cast as the blackguard of the piece.

'Derek was so uncompromising with the children. For some time, he would not even allow them to visit. He clung to this wretched argument that it was quite immoral for them to see their mother living with her "fancy man". Madeline was furious both that she was being prevented from communicating with her children on a regular basis and also with the business of the divorce.'

For Madeline, her marriage with the famous athlete had come to an inevitable end: 'I still have a lot of respect for Derek in some ways because he was always very good at home with the children. But I was entirely opposed to an attitude which seemed to say, "you go on having your affairs and I'll go on having my affairs". I have never countenanced that and never will. That is the basis of my relationship with Jonah.'

Such was the closeness of the bond between Nasrullah Khan and Barrington, between coach and pupil, that Barrington in effect had become Nasrullah Khan's adopted son. So the Madeline affair was something Nasrullah viewed with the utmost distaste. Madeline realised that Naz was wonderful to Jonah but she couldn't find anything likeable about him from the start. 'I remember when we went to the Edgbaston Priory Club to meet Naz. He was very off-hand; his attitude was that he had been neglected – that Jonah had forsaken him for me. He didn't want to talk to me but I went straight up to him. I tried to explain how much I did understand Jonah's needs because I had been an athlete, but at the end of the day it was quite clear that we hadn't solved anything as far as Naz was concerned.'

It was inevitable that the day Barrington met a woman he wanted to marry his close relationship with Nasrullah Khan would be affected. Sadly the proud Pakistani was never able to overcome his resentment that the man he regarded as his son was no longer under his control. Warning signs of what was to come were already evident in 1967. By that time, Jonah was no longer the 'skinny drip in glasses' whom Mike Corby had met three years earlier. He had won both the British Open and British Amateur twice and had acquired both the well-muscled body and the mental confidence of a top athlete. He knew that he was in demand for what he was – an effortlessly charming, well-mannered, articulate, good-looking world champion. But Nasrullah was never able to adapt to the person he was largely responsible for creating. Undoubtedly, Jonah was now his own man. Although he was sensible enough to realise that he did not know everything, he was fully aware that he did not need an advisory service that encroached on his entire life.

Victory alone was no longer enough for Jonah and the more he became aware of the imbalance in his life, the more resentful he became towards those whom he felt were responsible for his isolation. He had to remain world champion but he also knew that marriage and family life were vital to his future; and he now saw no reason why the two could not go together. The monk had at last decided to leave the monastery. The growing resentment that had been simmering between the squash player and his coach finally erupted when Madeline entered Jonah's life in 1969. 'It was just jealousy,' says Jonah. 'There was no blazing row but Naz was visibly disapproving of everything I did. The most vivid example of this – it shocked everybody – was following my defeat of Hunt in the Open at Abbeydale in 1972. I thought I had done rather well. After all, I had not scored a point for 27 minutes, I had been 7–0 down in the fifth and yet I had won. But when I left the court, Naz grabbed me by the shoulders, and glared at me. "You were so slow in the squash court," he said. The anger in his face was phenomenal.'

Nicholas Barrington clearly recalls that evening in 1972 for he had been delegated to look after the truculent Pakistani: 'We went out for a curry after the match. Nasrullah was drinking heavily, which was most untypical at that time, and the more he drank, the more bellicose he became. He just glared at everyone from his end of the table.' Jonah, too, remembers that there was trouble with Nasrullah that evening: 'He was so angry because he wasn't the centre of attention, or even near it. I had told Madeline that, whatever happened, win or lose, the first thing I was going to do afterwards was have a nice cold pint of beer. When I went into the bar after the match and Madeline gave me the pint, the dislike on his face for her and the whole episode was obvious.'

It was one of Jonah's most fervent wishes that Nasrullah

would accept Madeline and come to terms with the changed situation. But Nasrullah's fierce pride never allowed a reconciliation. Even some time later, when he had moved near the Barringtons, and Jonah asked if he was interested in taking him for a session a week, Nasrullah replied curtly that he was too busy. But while he was too busy even to meet the man he had helped become a world champion, he was regularly on court with Peter Webb, the man whose flat Jonah and Madeline had stayed in when they first came to the Birmingham area, having hour-long hitting sessions . . . 'feeding' sessions that Jonah had never had with Naz. Some years later, however, he was to learn that many times Naz's hand had hovered over the telephone wanting to put matters to rights . . . but his pride had never allowed him to make that one, all-important call.

Nasrullah Khan died in 1977 at the tragically early age of fifty-seven, and Jonah will for ever remain deeply conscious of the fact that they never settled their differences. 'Naz's son, Aman, of whom Madeline and I are very fond, rang me to break the news. I was utterly devastated but I made it clear that if there was anything I could do for my old mentor, I wanted to do it. And so it was that some days later I had the painful privilege of being a senior at his funeral in the Birmingham mosque. I loved him more than anyone could have loved him; I had been his son and I wept that I had not tried harder to resolve our differences before his death.' But Barrington will never forget the proud Pathan who all those years ago had ordered him to hit a squash ball 100 times up the forehand wall and then the backhand wall: 'I will always have a deep affection for Naz even though I was saddened that he was unable to accept someone who became particularly precious to me. I owe him an eternal debt and I will always remember all that he taught me. In that sense, he is still my mentor.'

9. The Broken-Down Hero

Despite his happy marriage to Madeline, Jonah again found himself standing in the shadows in 1973 when his mother finally succumbed to the ravages of cancer after suffering months of torment at Marratons.

Jonah was now 32. He had achieved his ambition to become a world champion, winning the British Open title six times. He had been such a successful evangelist on behalf of the sport that every week it seemed a new squash club was opening with members inspired by his example. True he was still driven by the incentive of equalling Hashim Khan's record of seven British Open titles, but other players had by now followed the Barrington example and begun to make life difficult on the tournament scene. The years of attrition and sacrifice had taken their toll on Barrington's mind and body and his mother's death was almost the last straw.

Jonah spent the final painful months of his mother's life at Marratons where he and Madeline nursed her as best they could, being joined regularly by Geraldine whenever she was able to get to Cornwall. 'Mother had never really complained about anything in her life so that when she said she was suffering, I knew she must be in dreadful pain. I remember late one night calling the doctor out from Bude, eight miles away. He just told us to give her the pain killers. I rang again at three in the morning but nobody came. It was the most terrible night and, about five in the morning, she said to me: "You know Jo, if I had known this is what I was going to suffer I would never have smoked one cigarette." I was later told categorically that smoking was the primary cause of both my father's and my mother's deaths and, what's more, I've been told my own skin tissue is likely to be the same as my mother's, so it is only sensible that my brother, sister and I have never smoked.'

Although Jonah was careful to keep fit with long runs around the rugged Cornish countryside, the mental shock of his mother's death was intense. As Madeline says, 'The rot set in after his mother died. He was very strong throughout the six months of her illness and on the day of the funeral he was amazingly controlled. I didn't see him break down or shed any tears but I knew how deeply he felt her loss, and soon he started to have a bad time sleeping, his training slackened and his health began to decline visibly.'

A shrewd and perceptive woman, Madeline recalls an incident that convinced her that cracks were beginning to appear in Jonah's façade. 'One day we had an argument over something pretty trivial. I stormed out to the shops but when I came back I found he had gone to bed. I went up to him and he was sobbing and really in a terrible state. It was such a shock seeing him like that. I couldn't understand why he had got so worked up. He explained that, with his mother gone, if we ever broke up he would literally have nothing. So I made a conscious effort to be very careful over the next few weeks. But it was heart-rending to see him going through so much grief; he dreamed about his mother almost constantly and became very emotional.'

It was clear that Barrington was fast becoming aware that although squash had given him almost everything, it had also in a sense left him with nothing. Almost a decade had passed since Jonah had set off on the single-minded pursuit of excellence that had now depleted his mental and physical resources. Since Trinity College and the years that followed, Jonah's spartan training routines and his avoidance of drink had meant that his social life had been virtually non-existent before he met Madeline. Nasrullah had been right in ensuring that Jonah was never deflected from his path, but under his austere régime there had been too little time for Jonah to relax. By 1973, therefore, the squash court had begun to be a prison rather than a stage on which he could dominate the world. But if that was so, Jonah was his own gaoler and it was his choice whether to stay or go; and his decision was made harder for he had begun to find that lonely practice sessions were not ideal therapy for a troubled mind.

Jonah himself was aware that the walls were coming in on him: 'I had been doing these routines for nearly a decade and I needed a break. But I could never let up because there would always be one big event or another to consider. With mother's death on my mind, I really couldn't face being alone on court, and if I was I would just run through the motions. I was fully aware of this, so, to offset the guilt, I would run. In fact I ran excessively and though I felt a great deal better afterwards, I would pretend to myself that I had done a really good day's work; it was pure therapy. By the end of that time I was exceedingly fit but in no way properly prepared to play world-class squash.'

Nevertheless, Jonah decided to embark on a 15-match tour with Cam Nancarrow, who had just turned professional. He knew it would be good preparation for the 1974 Open and it would certainly be better than practising by himself. He hoped it would also help to take his mind off his mother's death. At least that was the plan . . .

Cam, together with his wife, Mavis, and his stepson were staying with us, which was not a success. The atmosphere in the house became less pleasant by the day. I will always remember that, just to get a bit of privacy, Madeline and I went off to watch Birmingham City play Leeds. In a way, it suddenly seemed quite amusing to us that we had to be among 35,000 people just to get some privacy. Cam stayed with us until about ten days before the championship but all through that period he was unable to play because, in practice, he had run into the court wall, slipped, and damaged his big toe joint. For three weeks he couldn't play at all. He just sat in the bungalow with his foot up on the chair. I was getting up very early to train and going back to bed before getting up and going out again, yet all the time he sat there watching me with a wry smile on his face. It really was a very difficult time. Many people knew

131

that my mother's death had hit me hard, but Madeline and I realised that the other factor that had unsettled me was having Cam and Mavis living in our home.

For his part, Nancarrow found that staying with the Barringtons was a strange experience. 'One day Jonah was thrashing around doing his exercises when the phone rang. He picked it up, shouted "EXERCISES", and slammed it down again. If the phone ever rang late at night, he would shout "RUDE, RUDE, RUDE" at it.'

Jonah's problems with Nancarrow, on top of his mother's death, left him strained and depressed. He was still doing long training runs but his nerves were stretched to breaking point. 'It showed in his play,' recalls Madeline. 'When his arm went up to hit the ball you could see it shaking. You could actually *see* the tension.' Jonah had developed a condition that squash players regard with dread. Known as 'elbow', it makes it almost impossible to play any shot with confidence. Jonah's only relief now lay in sleeping pills. 'Previously I'd suffered from tension but I'd never had a problem sleeping . I'd always slept before tournaments, not well but satisfactorily. I should have taken things easier after mother died but I went beyond the limit. I even did three sessions on the day before the Open started. I must have been mental. I began taking an enormous number of sleeping pills, yet I'd never taken a sleeping pill in my life before mother's death. But for about two-and-a-half years afterwards I was on four Mogadons a night. It only came home to me when Madeline told me that I would never regain my psychological strength until I'd won the battle with those sleeping pills.'

Barrington was finally cured of the sleeping-pill habit on a subsequent visit to South Africa. Having lost to Kenny Hiscoe, he was on his way back to his hotel room and, with no one about, vented his anger and frustration at another defeat by, in his own words, 'Kicking shit out of the lift'. In the bath later, he noticed that his big toe had swollen considerably. A doctor was sent for. 'We were talking in general terms and this sleeping pill thing came up. I told him what I had been taking and he almost fell off his chair. He said it had to stop there and then and that I was doing myself a great deal of harm. He was so alarmed that I agreed to do what he said. I didn't take one that night, didn't sleep. I didn't take one the next night, didn't sleep. I roared into him after two sleepless nights and told him that while my toe was getting better, the rest of me felt bloody awful. He said I was suffering from withdrawal symptoms and put me on a weaker strain of pills and I was able to beat it in about a week.' (During the summer of 1973 he had travelled to South Africa and had had the upsetting experience of reading a newspaper article that said he was coming to play squash while his mother was dying. At the time he related it to the overall insensitivity in the country but 'it made me very belligerent'.)

Barrington's mother had died in November 1973. The 1974 British Open took place in February. In between Barrington had to come to terms with his grief and cope with Cam Nancarrow's presence in his house, all the while keeping up his fitness with those long gruelling runs. There is no doubt at all that when he travelled up to Abbeydale to defend his title he was better prepared to run in a cross-country championship than to play in the world's leading squash tournament – and he might have enjoyed it more. And psychologically he was a mess, relying on a nightly diet of sleeping pills. But the press and the public were largely unaware of his problems and it was confidently predicted that the Open was simply another confrontation between Jonah and Geoff Hunt, with Barrington about to equal Hashim's record. Unimpressive victories over Pat Kirton 9–1, 9–4, 9–6 and John Easter 9–6, 10–9, 10–9 earned Jonah a quarter-final place and a match with Mo Yasin, a man Barrington had always beaten previously, although he was always a difficult opponent, for he was tough and as fast as a cat. He was a man who had not been given a liberal measure of life's advantages, even by Pakistani standards: a background to make a man aware of an opportunity when it came his way. But no one in the squash world – except perhaps Madeline – was prepared for Jonah's defeat, 9–1, 4–9, 8–10, 2–9: 'I just had a feeling that it might be a difficult match. My form had been very poor, I felt far more strained than usual. I'll always remember trying to get my contact lenses in that day. It took me about ten minutes and my fingers were fiddling about all over the place. I suspect that I was pretty close to the limit by the time I went on court with Yasin.'

As the game proceeded there was little sign of the drama that was about to unfold. Although Jonah won the first game in no time at all, there was no sign of Nasrullah during the interval. In an attempt to 'psyche out' Jonah, the Pakistanis had set up a cordon of their players and officials around the court so that Nasrullah, who had agreed to advise Jonah during the match, was unable to get through. Jonah lost the second game but had game ball in the third before hitting a backhand out of court to lose it 8–10. Even then the old hands around the court were not particularly perturbed as they had seen Barrington claw his way back to victory from far more precarious situations and against far more formidable opposition than this. But precarious situations demand total concentration and that was something that was beyond Jonah that particular day. 'I had always been a pressure player. I played my best squash when I was behind, fighting, coming back. But I broke against Yasin, I came crashing down. Although I had a golden opportunity to wrap it up because I was one up and he was playing poorly, I began to play so badly that I let him back into the match. I should have had the third game but I didn't, and then he produced a series of extraordinary shots at the start of the fourth and soon he was too far ahead. I had felt absolutely shattered at the end of the third game.'

'I too felt tired at the end of the third,' recalls Mo Yasin, who won the match after taking the fourth game 9–2. 'But then I recovered. In my mind was the knowledge that he was after Hashim's title and I didn't want him to spoil Hashim's record.'

Nasrullah was in tears at the end of the match, distressed at Jonah's defeat. With hindsight Jonah feels that Nasrullah could have made it through the phalanx of Pathans blocking his path. 'Nasrullah was Nasrullah and every Pakistani was in awe of him,' says Jonah. 'He could have got through if he had wanted to.'

If the Pakistanis had been allowed to select a player to do a demolition job on an insecure Jonah, they couldn't have chosen better than Mohammed Yasin. He has the impassive demeanour of a gunfighter and even dresses like one with his cowboy boots, jeans and sheepskin coat. He lived up to his tough appearance that day, too, for having suffered a reversal in the first game he decided that Barrington needed softening up. In the second and third games he went straight in on Jonah's back with his knee and hit him five times with the ball. Rex Bellamy, in *The Times*, described it as: 'A tally of intimidating incidents that exceeds any reasonable law of averages.' Jonah, who has often said that squash was boxing with rackets, was not surprised at Yasin's physical onslaught: 'I'd been dishing it out to him over the years so it didn't upset me.'

So Hashim's record was safe and if anyone was to equal or beat it then it certainly wouldn't be Jonah. For, following the Yasin match, it was obvious that his psychological ascendancy over his fellow-professionals was gone for ever. And they knew it. Significantly he was also nearly 33, a fact that, prior to this defeat, was entirely without relevance. After all, it is not until an athlete starts to lose that the public begins to take much notice of his age. Furthermore, Jonah's back was now developing problems, which meant that for the next two-and-a-half years he would be unable to sleep on a normal bed. More importantly, this also robbed him of that pelvic suppleness without which the top player is at a terrible disadvantage. There was one further reason why Jonah's setback at the hands of Yasin was permanent and that was the emergence of Mohibullah Khan and Qamar Zaman. Azam Khan, employing the same methods he had used on Jonah nearly a decade earlier, once again worked his magic on these two Pakistanis and Barrington found himself unable to respond to this new challenge. From 1974 onwards, he faced the awesome prospect of encountering either of these two wizards at the quarter-final stage of every major tournament, while Geoff Hunt, being seven years younger than Jonah, was able to draw on resources that were much fresher.

It is not without irony that Barrington was closer to retirement in 1974 than he is today. Indeed a lesser man would probably have thrown in the towel there and then. The loss of his Open title and the emergence of Zaman and Mohibullah came closest to putting him out to grass. These were bitter times for Jonah and it took six weeks on the beach in Mombasa, soothed by the sun and the warm trade winds, to heal his wounds. 'I was a wreck after that defeat,' he admits.

It has often been said that I suffer from verbal diarrhoea and it's true I never stopped talking after that championship. Madeline told me, 'Shut up, for heaven's sake, you must shut up, everybody's looking at you as if you're going to flip.' But I couldn't stop talking. I had to get it out of my system, I suppose. But Kenya was the best possible rehabilitation I could have had. Running along the beach, with a few beers at night at the Trade Winds Hotel thinking about things, I realised that if I was to continue playing and not retire, then I would have to practise regularly on court again. So, with my mind made up, we returned to England and I got in touch with Bomber Harris.

From 1974 to 1981, Jonah's main priority would be to maintain a world ranking somewhere between five and eight. And paradoxically, the older he got, the more his results improved. In 1978 he beat Mohibullah Khan in the Singapore Open and two years later beat an emerging Jahangir Khan first in the quarter-final of the British Open and then again in the final of the Irish Open when he played so well he would have beaten anyone. He also put his reputation as the country's leading player on the line in the British Closed Championship that year, but he destroyed his nearest rival, Gawain Briars, 3–1, playing marvellous squash after a hesitant start. But what Jonah did not like during this period was the merciless on-court approach of the big four – Hunt, Zaman, Mohibullah and Hiddy Jahan – and the obvious satisfaction they derived in reducing him to

136

a dribble of sweat. Hunt relished the opportunity and now that he had finally achieved a physical and psychological ascendancy over Jonah he was never to let up:

> When I began to deteriorate he became absolutely ruthless. He knew I was suffering and he would grind me in unmercifully. Yet I would watch him playing some palooka whom he could easily have beaten 3–0 in 30 minutes and he would play a carefree relaxed match and win 3–1. The following day he would come out against me and beat me 3–0 in 75 minutes for the loss of eight points, without playing a shot from behind except a boast. I suppose it was a compliment to me, because he still felt I was a danger, but it was a compliment I could have done without.
>
> In the last part of my Open career everyone treated me as if I was potential world champion. Against Zaman I never had a moment's grace. No one gave me the first game by playing casually. I always wanted to get my rhythm and then the first game. Then I could go to four games, and the longer a game went on, the better my chance, because no one, except Geoff Hunt, trained as hard as I did. The only difference between Geoff and me was that he was doing monstrous training sessions and winning the British Open, whereas I was doing monstrous training sessions and not winning the British Open.

Jonah's resentment towards the manner in which the top four or five players now gleefully pounded him in is a good example of the macabre logic that sometimes confuses his thinking. Did Corby, Taleb, Jawaid, Hiscoe or Alauddin ever enjoy the luxury of a casual first game against him when *he* was champion? 'Well, no, they never did,' admits Jonah, laughingly aware that it might be asking a little too much of his opponents to adopt a merciful approach towards him when he himself had never displayed such qualities. It is ironic, therefore, that as a result of his own ruthless approach, which his opponents copied, Barrington had become the architect of his own destruction.

10. 'I'll Get You Afterwards'

Jonah Barrington's great success as a squash player and innovator owed much to a volatile mind. Along with his restless energy, he also had a temper usually masked by his middle-class reserve. Never a man to endure for very long what he thought was wrong, that reserve would often evaporate whenever he launched one of his many controversial attacks on either the squash establishment, his critics or sometimes his fellow-players. And occasionally, he could completely lose control of his temper with spectacular results.

When Barrington was at his peak, only one other player apart from Geoff Hunt consistently had him in difficulties in major championships: the Australian left-hander Cam Nancarrow. The record books may not put them on the same high level; after all, Barrington won the British Open six times and the title was never achieved once by Nancarrow. But Nancarrow was sufficiently skilled to win the World Amateur Championships individual title in South Africa in 1973, and in the earlier part of his career he had beaten Barrington in two major tournaments. Furthermore Nancarrow had been primarily responsible for ensuring that Barrington's first visit to Australia in 1967 ended in total failure. Barrington had arrived in Australia as a sensation – the man who had come from nowhere to win the game's two most prized events, the British Open and the British Amateur Championships. But, as we have seen, his hopes of salvaging his poor playing record ended at Albert Park, Melbourne, when Nancarrow defeated him 9–7, 9–6, 9–7. From then on Nancarrow was to be more than a thorn in Barrington's side for in January 1969 at Abbeydale, Sheffield, he put paid to the Cornishman's hopes of winning the British Open title for the third consecutive time, defeating him 9–4, 9–5, 10–8 in the semi-finals.

During the late 1960s, the press were to describe the rather ungainly six-foot Australian as 'Jonah's Jinx' and the battles between them were never a particularly good advertisement for the game. Nancarrow, in contrast to Barrington, was always seeking to end a rally by employing his impressive racket skills and, in the words of Rex Bellamy, he was a superb nick player: 'The difference between Nancarrow and most of his breed lies in his flexible wrist work and the kind of winners he produces. He uses a lot of drops, angles and reverse angles and flicks the ball on and off the side walls in a way that tampers with the conventional geometry of a squash shot. His touch is so good that he is always dangerous when allowed to drift to the front of the court.'

Barrington's great problem against Nancarrow was that he so often found himself trapped behind the Australian's awkward body, denied direct access to the ball, or indeed a clear view of it. This added to the conflict in their styles and, additionally, the fact that they were both left-handers produced erratic contests forever disrupted by endless numbers of lets and penalty points.

In Bellamy's view, Barrington and Nancarrow were destined to create the equivalent of a squash-court traffic jam – their play was a complete conflict of styles and intentions, aesthetically displeasing and unworkable: 'Nancarrow was a little bit flat-footed, never the nimblest person getting off the mark, and this could very often be construed as obstruction, which it wasn't. Jonah always had the problem of whether he should try to go around Cam or ask for a let, especially on the backhand wall.' The players' opinions of each other, however, were usually expressed in less gentlemanly terms. In Barrington's eyes, Nancarrow was taking gamesmanship beyond the rules and the Australian, in his turn, was never that complimentary about Barrington's on-court behaviour during their battles. He always thought Jonah crowded him instead of standing back and using his speed and fitness to get around him to the ball.

By the 1970s, however, Nancarrow was no longer 'Jonah's Jinx', for the Cornishman fought back resolutely. After that Abbeydale defeat, Barrington routed Nancarrow in straight games, 9–0, 9–2, 10–8, in the semi-finals of the 1969 World Amateur Championships individual event. And just to drive the message home, he was to win his personal series with the Australian that winter, despite at one stage being 2–5 down. But Nancarrow remained a very difficult opponent and Barrington always found their matches intensely frustrating. By the middle of the 1970s, Barrington was battling hard with the reality that he was no longer winning major tournaments. And his troubles were hardly soothed each time he met Nancarrow on court – twice in South Africa the resentment that had been building up for years finally erupted out of control.

When the professional circuit was making its way around South Africa in the mid-1970s the gallery of spectators at one Barrington–Nancarrow battle was staggered to realise that the Cornishman had decided that his opponent's backside was a far more interesting target than the ball. 'The one thing he was determined not to give me was continuity; he would achieve some part of his objective with his racket but the greater part with his body. Admittedly I compounded what he was doing by playing too close to him. I couldn't get through to the ball and he argued that I was crowding him. During this particular rally, I just continued with my racket on the backhand in a rather spectacular swing and gave him a beautiful set of strings across his backside. I couldn't resist the target. Everybody in the gallery fell over laughing and the referee was silent for about thirty seconds. Then after saying "Good Heavens" a few times, he allowed the match to continue.'

Nancarrow remembers Barrington 'playing like a maniac that day. It was a typical situation. He played a loose shot. I played a drop shot and I was slightly forward to the right of the T. He said something about a fat arse and hit me with the top of his racket. In the heat of the match it didn't hurt very much; it was like being hit by the ball. But I was very annoyed. I gave him a good solid push with both hands, after which we cooled down and continued playing.' Not unreasonably, the Australian world champion, Geoff Hunt, thought that Barrington should have been thrown off the court after the incident, but the game continued.

Hunt, remembering that a passing drive caused the problem, viewed the incident as another example of the eccentric streak in Barrington's character: 'Many of Jonah's problems were caused by the size of Nancarrow's backside masking the ball and the racket head. Jonah expected a drop shot and was passed by a drive. Instead of running back down the court to retrieve the ball, he took one step back and aimed a massive drive at Nancarrow's backside. It produced the most amazing bruise I have ever seen.'

This incident was, however, somewhat mild in comparison with another Barrington outburst when the two players toured South Africa again in 1976. As far as Jonah was concerned, the trouble started in Rhodesia:

We had played what was then the longest match in the history of squash at the Salisbury Sports Club. It was quite a bit longer than my match with Geoff Hunt at the Edgbaston Priory Club when I won the 1969 British Open. My game with Hunt lasted 2 hours and 13 minutes and there were about 12 lets. But in my match with Nancarrow we wallowed backwards and forwards for nearly 2½ hours and there must have been about 100 lets – possibly as many as 12 on one single point. It was horrendous. At one stage, he actually held on to my shorts and then he was literally talking on court into my ear, whispering things like 'You'll miss this one' and so on. I just stopped playing and turned to the referee: 'I'm not a telltale and never have been but *this joker is talking to me during the rallies*. I don't care what the rules are but this is just another form of his cheating.' Later when I was 7–6 ahead in the fifth, I knew that if I could hang on I'd got him. But, I'm not joking, he got a penalty point to regain his serve, he got a penalty point to level the scores at seven all, he got a penalty point to go 8–7 ahead and he got a penalty point to win the match 9–7 in the fifth. I couldn't believe it – four consecutive penalty points had been awarded against me. Nancarrow could hardly believe it either and he seemed embarrassed in the changing room not over the match, which had been total warfare, but over the unfair way the idiot up above had spoilt the whole show by awarding those penalty points.

When we went down to Johannesburg to play, it was obvious that I was very uptight. Psychologically it was a highly frustrating period for me. I felt I was up against the wall. We were playing at Witwatersrand University and very early on in the match he got up to what I call his tricks. He was getting his blocking tactics in. After he had won the first game and we went off court beneath the gallery, I gave him the biggest mouthful I have ever given any player between games. One or two people arriving late for the match would have heard my extraordinary outburst. I called him every name under the sun. In the second game, I was getting more and more out of control and any reserve I may have had disappeared. At the end of the game, I told him: 'You know what you are up to, you know exactly what you are doing and if I don't get you on court, you bastard, I'll get you ✶✶✶✶✶✶✶✶ afterwards.' He could have done anything in the third game, I didn't care. But then as soon as we got back to the changing room, I pitched straight in: 'Perhaps you think you're bloody smart, and perhaps you think you're bloody clever, but I'll show you just how smart you are.' And I went for him.

I chased him to the shower area and I got in with one or two hard punches, actually dislocating my thumb in the process. There I was effing and blinding, when an old friend of mine from Trinity days, Geoff Lemon, came in. Now Nancarrow was a lot bigger than me and I think Geoff probably thought he was going to kill me, so he intervened. But actually Nancarrow wasn't hitting back. I kept on trying to land one on him but he held me off. It must have been like a little Scotty dog trying to attack a Great Dane. We were in the shower area, which was a bit confined, and he must have had me by the neck. Anyway, eventually two or three people helped Geoff Lemon to stop the fight. I'm glad Geoff himself didn't have a go at Nancarrow because Geoff is a hard, nuggety Protestant Ulsterman. He had been a British Universities boxing champion and he was lethal.

I don't regret what I did. It was an utterly understandable outburst. I don't think Nancarrow ever appreciated the aggravation his play had caused me over the years. It would have been pathetic if I *hadn't* done something like that. My nature is such that I would have shown my temper at some stage or other and during this match I could contain myself no longer. It could just as easily have happened after the British Open in 1969.

At least the two men, despite their differences, have a sense of humour, and during the 1982 Audi World Championships at the National Exhibition Centre in Birmingham, Nancarrow could be found accepting a dinner invitation from the man who attacked him. And in his room at the Metropole Hotel during that visit to Britain, Nancarrow talked about the incident with that half-smile on his face with which Australians make even the most outlandish event seem almost a matter-of-fact occurrence. Yet Barrington's behaviour disturbed the Australian at the time:

As the years go by everything softens. But at the time I was revolted. If someone else had been there when he was getting those blows in, a lot more would have come of it. I would have taken him to court on an assault charge. I don't know if I would have won but it would have shown the world what a maniac he was.

I had decided that day to be nice to Jonah and keep out of his way. I clapped my racket when Jonah hit a nice shot and this had a terrible effect on Jonah. Perhaps I was being sarcastic but he had been like that for years, so I thought I would have a go back. In my opinion we had a clean game – we only collided a couple of times. But when I got back to the changing room, he started raving: he had that glazed look. He shouted that I had been annoying him for years and he was going to hit me. This bloke was in front of me grabbing me in a bear hug, so Jonah had trouble connecting. But he certainly landed a few blows. Then I grabbed his neck. I've got a long reach and after I got hold of him he couldn't really hit me properly. But he was mouthing these obscenities all the time, shouting 'You bastard, you've been doing it for years.' We were falling all over the changing room – it must have been an extraordinary scene – but the fight was stopped after about three minutes. Jonah's eyeballs were popping out. He was absolutely raving.

Extreme though Jonah's behaviour was, others also found playing Nancarrow a frustrating experience. In the view of Australian Ken Hiscoe, 'Everyone knows he got away with murder for years.' Jonah can recall Geoff Hunt reporting Nancarrow to referees for timewasting. For example, on his service, he would deliberately serve a fault down the wrong side of the court out of his opponent's reach. Hunt also remembers Ken Hiscoe, beating Nancarrow at Wembley in the quarter finals of the 1975 British Open Championship: 'In the final rally, Hiscoe was on match-point and almost there when one of Nancarrow's shoes came off. Hiscoe kept one eye on the shoe and the other on Nancarrow, determined not to give him a chance of winning the point. Finally he did win the point and the match, with Nancarrow spreadeagled out unable to reach the ball. Ken was over the moon; he had actually nailed him. Nancarrow was livid; he refused to shake hands and then stopped Hiscoe getting out of the court by appealing in vain for a let with his arms akimbo across the court door. It was all most unseemly.'

Fortunately perhaps, the ugly changing-room fracas was never made public, but in 1975, in front of millions of television viewers, Barrington's temper erupted again. He was competing in the highly popular BBC series *International Superstars*, which brought together top sportsmen of all types to compete in various events. When his invitation had arrived, Jonah had accepted readily, seeing the competition as a splendid opportunity to further the cause of squash. Having earned a reputation as one of the fittest men in the world, he was determined to win. But there were to be serious problems:

In 1975, I was having trouble with my back, I'd also lost the British Open for the second year in a row and I was really going through the mill, wondering if I was on the decline and what the hell I was going to do about it. Years earlier I had tried to make it obvious that I would be very interested in doing a *Superstars*. In the early series, I felt I had a reasonably good chance of doing very well, but when no offer to appear arrived I grew increasingly frustrated; it really was something I wanted to do. Finally in 1975 a few hints were dropped that I might be invited and, on the basis of that alone, I began training. I knew what the events were. I had watched the previous series and made notes. So I got a bike, I kicked a football and the squat-thrusts were the things I used to do in training with Bomber Harris. I knew I was going to be pretty well prepared if the call came, but what really angered me was that no one would tell me when the event was likely to take place.

That summer, at long last, I was told that in all probability, I was going to be in *Superstars*, and as every European heat was held in a different country, it looked likely that I would be going to Spain. So I waited patiently all through the summer, not knowing for certain when or where I might be competing, but nevertheless training hard for every event. When the South African circuit began, I had to go off there, but I kept up my training. I ran round a local stadium, rode my bike on a tartan track – at least until I hit a sneaky brick one day and found myself flying through the air – I practised shooting on a range – plum next to a dynamite factory – and relentlessly kicked football penalties with Bomber Harris and the former England youth goalkeeper, Barry Dennis, both of whom I had brought with me.

A few weeks later we were in Rhodesia when the call finally came and I knew that I was in. But it wasn't San Sebastian, it wasn't Nice, it wasn't even Calais, it was Aldershot, the home of the British Army! At once, though, I pulled out of two squash tournaments, bought a £500 air ticket and flew home. I arrived only a day and a half before the competition began and, knowing how weak my shooting was, I was determined to get some practice. But would you credit it, in Aldershot of all places I couldn't get hold of so much as a starting pistol? I was pretty mad about that, especially as the Army had taken full advantage of my presence by getting me to play at least six members of their squash team. So I was stymied, and reduced to kicking a ball around with Bomber, playing tennis and doing my exercises.

The next morning the competition got under way. I was surprisingly edgy as I knew that I was representing my sport and not just myself.

As it happened, there was a real joker in the pack, the Swedish pole vaulter, Kjell Isaksson, who went on to win almost every competition he appeared in. Quite soon I realised that there was no chance I would win my heat but that I might come second and get to the final on a points basis. I had a pretty good first day, winning the tennis, that was no problem. I didn't take part in the 100 yards as I can't sprint, but I came second to the Swede in the weights. So, for me, the last event of the day was the most critical – the squat-thrusts. We were up on a raised platform with a British Army physical training instructor acting as counter. I reckoned he was thinking we were all over-paid little idiots and why wasn't he allowed to show what he could do as he could do more tricep dips than any of the contestants. Anyway, off we went. I had done thousands of squat-thrusts in my training sessions with Bomber Harris and I knew that on a bad day I could do a minimum of 75 – the record was then held by the boxer John Conteh with about 81. I was going like the clappers. I knew I had probably done better than anyone else, but while I was thrusting away I could hear the army guy muttering away behind me, and when we finished he gave me 25. I was enraged as I had clearly put in maximum effort and must have got 70-odd at least. I protested at once and there was a furious scene. The cameras went on shooting and I am told there was some interesting footage of a belligerent discussion between me and the pentathlete Jim Fox, the former Rugby player Campbell-Lamerton, and David Vine, the compère. I had to be physically restrained from assaulting Fox and Campbell-Lamerton, which would have been stupid as they were rather bigger than me. I flung my Adidas bag through the air – apparently one of the best advertisements ever for the sports goods company – and trooped back to the hotel with Bomber and Barry Dennis. I don't think anybody had seen a televised tantrum before. I had never been so publicly angry in my life. Back at the hotel, we had a council-of-war. Barry Dennis said 'Up 'Em,' Bomber said 'Up 'Em' and I said 'Up 'Em.' I decided I would fly back next morning to South Africa and my prime business of playing the South African circuit.

As Bomber Harris was coming out of Jonah's room he met Ken Hawkes, one of the *Superstars* organisers, in the corridor.

'Everything okay now? Jonah okay?' asked Hawkes.

'Fine,' said Bomber smiling happily. 'He's on the nine o'clock flight in the morning to Jo'burg.' And on he marched pursued by an open-mouthed Hawkes.

'What do you mean?' asked Hawkes.

'He's booked on the 9.15 to Jo'burg, or maybe it's 9 o'clock,' said Bomber.

'But what about tomorrow?'

'Don't get me wrong, mate,' said Bomber. 'But he's booked on the 9 o'clock to Jo'burg.'

A few minutes later a very worried Hawkes was knocking on Jonah's door. 'I told him there was no way I was going to put up with that sort of ruling and that was that. There were many hurriedly convened conferences, until finally there was a 2 am meeting in my room where all the production teams, including those from Europe, materialised. They told me that if I dropped out I would always regret what I had done. I said that as far as I was concerned there were real sports waiting to be played and *Superstars* wasn't one of them. They all thought I would change my mind but they were wrong. I was on that plane the next morning as I had intended. It was an expensive decision, though. I was fined heavily for missing the two tournaments and with the air tickets, plus Bomber's and Barry's expenses, my part in *Superstars* had cost me well over £2000.'

Malcolm Hamer, by now Barrington's agent, wasn't too enthusiastic about the whole business either: '*Superstars* then was just a diversion, an entertainment for top sportsmen. Jonah entered in order to win, and for all the right reasons; he wanted to put squash fully on the map, and full marks to him. But he got it totally and utterly out of proportion. When I collected him at the airport, he wanted to know why I had not done this and that and he didn't stop complaining for a second. For the first time in my life, I came close to thumping a client. My own view is he was on the verge of a nervous breakdown. He was completely wrong about the ruling and he lost control. I was surprised he pulled out because it was so unprofessional – and so untypical – of him. Jonah has always been good on television and this was so out of character.'

Some months later, Jonah saw the transmission of the programme and realised at once that he had been in the wrong. 'I could see quite clearly that I had not done the exercise properly; in fact I shouldn't have been given any points at all, let alone 25! What had happened was that I had stiffened up throughout the day and by the time we reached the squat-thrusts, I just wasn't moving freely. I wasn't getting the knees to the elbows as the rules demanded and so they were entirely justified in marking me as they did.'

The following year, 1976, to his great surprise, Jonah was again invited to take part in *Superstars*, and again at short notice, but this time he agreed readily, decided to enjoy himself and came sixth out of ten. And every time he was interviewed, he beamed broadly and said what a great time he was having and not to worry, he'd still be around the next morning!

Nevertheless he still feels rather bitter about the whole *Superstars* business. 'When I had a telephone call from Malcolm to say that I had been invited back again, I said, "You're joking." But no, it was genuine. So I asked "When?", only to be told, "Tomorrow." That was in a sense their revenge. But whenever the *Superstars* incident is mentioned, my immediate reaction is that I was in the wrong. Unlike most politicians, I can always face up to that.'

11. And Then There Was Light

'Before Barrington, there were cobwebs on the courts of Pakistan. If you stopped somebody in the street and asked him what squash was, he would have said Robinsons make it and it comes in a bottle. Jonah Barrington was the man who created the squash boom . . . in this country, anywhere in the world. His contribution to the game is greater than any man's . . . I would not even give that statement a second thought.'

Thus says the *Daily Telegraph* squash correspondent, Dicky Rutnagur, a sportswriter who followed Barrington's career throughout the world ever since he first became headline news in the mid-1960s. Some would argue that his is an exaggerated viewpoint. John Horry, former secretary of the Squash Rackets Association and an important figure in the history of the sport, believes that a squash boom in Britain was inevitable: 'Squash is such a marvellous game. You get your exercise in such a short time, it's cheap and is not affected by the weather. It was starting to take off in the 1930s but suffered a frightful setback with the war. Then after the war, there was a shortage of building materials and the sport was forced to stagnate until it was possible to start building courts. I realised there was going to be a squash boom but I never thought it would come so quickly. Barrington did an awful lot to start the ball rolling and he was certainly very lucky that he rose to the heights at just the right time. We needed a world champion and he caught the imagination of the public. In my opinion half his battle was won because his name was Jonah – it is such an unusual name. If his name had been John, nobody would have taken much notice.'

Undoubtedly Barrington was helped by his unusual Christian name, yet other minor British sports had produced world champions and had still remained minor sports. Before his arrival, squash was an obscure game played by ex-public schoolboys. In 1965, before Barrington had fought his way to the top, there were 425 squash clubs in England and only 910 courts. But his personality, lifestyle and unusual name, coupled with the fact that he was a world champion, provoked unprecedented interest and people who had never set foot on a squash court or even held a racket turned to the sport in their thousands and, as keeping fit became increasingly fashionable, businessmen up and down the country ventured into squash courts determined to ward off the effects of middle-age. Through Barrington, the game enjoyed a degree of publicity previously unheard of. Not only was there regular coverage in newspapers such as *The Times*, the *Daily Telegraph* and the *Guardian* but suddenly popular newspapers such as the *Daily Mirror* began to show an unprecedented interest and there was only one explanation: Jonah Barrington. He was such an unusual character. Not only could he talk eloquently, he was not afraid to express his point of view. He had clearly stated his resolve to become the best squash player in the universe; he was determined to put a gap as wide as the Atlantic Ocean between himself and all those blasted Australians and Pakistanis; it was he who put up £1,500 of his own money to bring the Australian Geoff Hunt to Britain to prove just who was the best player in the world; he was the lone individual who dared to attack the traditional British 'Play Up and Play the Game' attitude with its emphasis on flair and little else; and he it was who accused the SRA of living in the Dark Ages and fought to push the game into the present and become open. With a squash racket in his hand, he was the super-fit sportsman fighting an endless war of attrition, playing a percentage game, keeping the ball in play, wearing down his opponents. But off the court, he showed great flair, vision and a sense of humour. He made such good copy that the press could hardly ignore him and once he had attracted the limelight, he remained in it because, despite all his faults and inconsistencies, he was always ready to be interviewed by the press or to go in front of the television cameras.

Rex Bellamy first came across Barrington when he was not

even considered good enough to be anything more than a first-round loser in the major tournaments. But he was impressed by the young man's remarkable faith in himself:

> My feeling at the time was that Jonah was quite possibly the most exciting and remarkable sportsman I had ever met. I have been writing about sport since 1944 and have met many very remarkable people – Newcombe, Roche, Laver, Rosewall, Margaret Court, Heather McKay, Geoff Hunt – but I have never met anyone as remarkable as Jonah. I have met better athletes, better racket-handlers, I've met people with better minds, but I have certainly never met anyone with a stronger character or a stronger will.
>
> Jonah created the squash boom not only in this country but all over the world. The speed of the boom, the advent of open competition, professionalism, people earning a living from the game through coaching, squash as a valid segment of the entertainment industry – all this came from Jonah. One of the remarkable things about him is his ability to generate publicity. He was able to see three or four journalists in succession and give each one a different feature. He has an extraordinary facility for shifting his mind and has always been a fascinating evangelist for the game. He opened windows in one's mind and let fresh ideas come in. He is the most important figure in the entire history of the game.

The British squash explosion was a remarkable event; the somewhat esoteric nature of the sport being vividly illustrated by the fact that when the SRA was founded in 1929, there were only 28 member clubs with a mere 60 courts, the estimated total number of courts in England being no more than 160. Throughout the next ten years these numbers gradually increased, though the Second World War disrupted the game to such an extent that, by 1947, there were fewer clubs and fewer courts than there had been in 1938. But since the late 1940s the game has grown, the 1970s

152

producing the most dramatic transformation with the arrival of squash complexes. In the 1965–70 period, the number of SRA member-clubs rose from 425 to 600 and the total number of courts increased from 910 to 1,394. Furthermore, in the next decade, another 1,034 clubs opened and 4,863 courts were built. The entrepreneurs had at last realised that squash courts could hardly fail to be a financial success. And while many sportsmen and sportswomen merely used squash as an enjoyable way to keep fit, or as an alternative to jogging on wet winter mornings, the decade also witnessed the advent of large numbers of serious players and the rapid expansion of the competitive side of the game.

In the past few years, there has been a general view that the squash boom is over. But the SRA feels this is far from the case and has statistics to prove that the expansion has not slowed down. In 1980, a record 979 new courts were built in England, and today there are an estimated 8,000 courts of which 691 were built in 1982. And these are statistics born of a severe economic recession.

Bob Morris, a former RAF squadron leader, and now the SRA's chief executive, is certain of a considerable number of courts currently under construction, even though the ever-increasing SRA statistics do not signify that each additional court is necessarily a new one: 'Our own intelligence system is improving all the time so that sometimes we get to hear of courts tucked away in some village we never previously knew about. The highest rate of construction was in 1976, 1977 and 1978 when the number increased by an average of some 20 per cent. Some may say the boom is over but they base their argument on the fact that there are fewer big complexes being built. In the late 1970s, eight court complexes were being opened practically every other month. That has undoubtedly slowed down because the commercial clubs are finding the going so tough in the recession and some are even going into liquidation. With soaring building costs and interest rates rising to unprecedented levels, they discovered too late that they had crippling millstones around their necks. But court construction has continued at the same average rate as it has during the past decade. Many companies are now building courts for their employees, many schools are building courts, as are hotels and hockey and rugby clubs.'

Perhaps even more remarkable is the estimated number of people now playing the game. In December 1982, *Squash News*, the SRA's official newspaper, reported the surprising fact that 'Squash is now played on a regular basis in the United Kingdom by more people than both soccer and cricket – our two traditional "National Sports". 'The evidence for this came from two national surveys and *Squash News* produced the statistics that the top participation sport in the United Kingdom was swimming, with 9.1 million people, badminton was second with 4.2 million, and squash third with 2.8 million. Fourth equal were jogging and table tennis with 2.6 million, while soccer was near the bottom of the list with 1.9 million and cricket was the least popular of the ten sports surveyed with a mere 1.2 million. How ironic then that squash merited only an hour's television coverage in the first six months of 1982 while horse racing received 174 hours, snooker 107 hours, tennis 98 hours and soccer 111 hours; so much television time was devoted to darts that the magazine didn't bother to list a figure.

While there is no doubt that squash has become a major participant sport in Britain, a figure of 2.8 million regular players seems suspicious. Divide the number of players into the number of courts and the implication is that somewhere near a couple of hundred people are sharing a court for a year. As Morris says: 'Although they are perfectly valid surveys, we are always a little nervous about quoting these figures. All we can say is 2.8 million people have played the game. The figure is meant to represent regular players but it can't make sense if you consider the number of courts.'

The squash boom inspired by Barrington was to bring him high financial rewards, the kind of sums that past squash players would never have believed possible. His decision to turn professional in 1969 was accompanied by two symbolic gestures – he coached Naz for a guinea and sold Rex Bellamy a squash racket for a shilling. It was an inevitable decision. There was no way he could pursue a career in another field while continuing to train and play with the dedication that had made him a world champion. But how could he make a living out of the game? 'Money didn't worry me in the slightest. Very shortly after I became involved at the highest level I resolved to develop squash as a career. But people thought it was a joke. Since there was no prize money worth talking about, how could anyone develop squash into a career?'

The major problem originally facing Barrington was an absence of adequate competitive programmes for professionals. The British game had always centred on the amateur and although he was to succeed Nasrullah Khan as the professional at the Lansdowne Club, this was no more than a token appointment – 'I don't think I ever gave anyone a lesson; they knew I would be away for much of the time.' He campaigned to make the game open and surprised the squash hierarchy by taking part in the Bath Cup knowing that, although no professionals had ever competed in it, there was no barring rule. And he sought to increase the number of world-class professionals so that a professional circuit could be formed to play all over the world. During 1969–70, Barrington himself paid a large sum to bring Geoff Hunt to Britain for a 15-match series, and even though he lost the series 13–2, the event put squash in the news. Nevertheless Barrington won the match that mattered that season – the British Open. In August 1970, with Aftab Jawaid, Rainer Ratinac, Sharif Khan and Abou Taleb, Barrington set off on a tour of Australia, the Middle East and the Far East, sponsored by Pakistan International Airlines, which, apart from its success in spreading the squash gospel to countries with little or no knowledge of the game, marked the beginning of the hugely successful professional squash circus.

Barrington, the man who opened windows in the mind, also developed a method of spreading the gospel of squash without the help of his fellow-professionals. The squash court became both his pulpit and the stage on which he could make full use of his considerable talents as a raconteur. Following the opening by the Duke of Edinburgh of the new £800,000 National Squash Centre at Wembley on 26 November 1974, a *Daily Express* headline declared: 'It's court jester Jonah'.

> Jonah Barrington staged his own Royal Command performance before the Duke of Edinburgh and the television cameras yesterday. The occasion was the opening of the Wembley championship court . . . Barrington came on court to face the game's largest live audience of over 400 people with a line in patter that would have done justice to Victor Borge.
>
> His 15-minute spot, officially reserved for a clinic on the game, turned into a Barrington talkie. He used his racket as Borge uses a piano, as an incidental, and had the audience rocking with his impressions of players.
>
> It was a performance that can do more for squash than 50 televised matches and hopefully the BBC will find time for coverage of the event either tonight on *Sportsnight*, or on Saturday in *Grandstand*.

But what that Wembley audience had seen was a snippet of a Barrington squash clinic. The idea had developed by accident in 1967 when Jonah had visited South Africa for a short exhibition tour on his way back to Britain from Australia. Although he had only been playing the game seriously for three years, officials told him enthusiastically: 'You're a talker, let's fill a gallery and you go on court and talk.' So with just a few days' notice Barrington went on to the main championship court at The Wanderers Club in Johannesburg and looked up to see hundreds of people gathered in the gallery waiting for him to speak. It was an interesting experience: 'I didn't know what the hell I was going to say. In detail, squash is a very boring game. How many ways can you tell people how to hit the ball on to that front wall? But I said to myself, you practise on your own, so tell them what you do. Tell them about the Khans and anything else that comes to mind. That was my first clinic and it was then that I realised there were other ways to be a successful squash professional than working for a club coaching and restringing rackets.'

The squash clinic provided the perfect method for Barrington to demonstrate his skills as a player and his flair for the anecdote. Squash clubs throughout Britain would fill their galleries with eager spectators and then Barrington, with perhaps a couple of guinea-pigs for practical demonstrations, would talk about his experiences and how Nasrullah Khan had explained the game and how, when he was world champion, he was always losing to Azam Khan, the ageing Pakistani at the New Grampians Club. And after the hour-long clinic, an exhibition match would follow against leading local players or the club professional. It was pure entertainment.

In the early 1970s, Barrington was paid about £75 for a clinic but today he justifies a considerably higher figure for what should be two hours' work but invariably goes on longer – evidence of his great appeal, for it is now more than a decade since he was world champion. As Mike Corby says: 'Jonah created a myth and he is still the greatest public relations man I have ever come across. He walks on court and is brilliant. No one I have ever met can talk about themselves for so long and have everybody loving every moment of it.' Bob Morris, chief executive of the SRA, saw his first Barrington clinic in Newcastle: 'They are a fairly hard-nosed bunch in that part of the world but Jonah has an aura about him. He was the classic entertainer with an ability to hold people just where he wanted them. He has the talent to do so many things well . . . he can speak seriously and thoughtfully, he can speak lightheartedly and flippantly, he can speak professionally about coaching. His presence, his eloquence and his engaging personality are a remarkable blend.'

When other leading players turned professional, Barrington became the prime mover behind the formation in 1973 of the International Squash Players Association.

After Ken Hiscoe, Geoff Hunt and Gogi Alauddin turned pro and other players were showing definite interest, I was determined to get some kind of pro circuit going. It finally took off through an event called The Prodorite which was staged at Edgbaston

157

Priory. They refused to do the draw as we wanted so we held a players' meeting and decided there and then to form the ISPA. It was clear that unless we were forever going to be at the mercy of tournament committees, international governing bodies, and so on, we had to get ourselves organised. What the tournament organisers had to appreciate was that if they wanted a top-class event, they would need us to play, so we were in the ultimate position of influence. That's when I evolved the idea of PPP – Proper Playing Power. It's not a blackmail situation – it's a situation where players have the power but must use it responsibly. Very early on we felt that the SRA were being obstructive and on a couple of occasions we all came perilously close to withdrawing from the British Open.

Everybody mistrusted ISPA at the start and quite honestly we *were* rather limited in some ways. Professionals are perhaps not the ideal people to run associations. I've been at the heart of ISPA since it started and that is perhaps one of the reasons why it has been a bit of a mess! I'm not saying that if I concentrated on administration and correspondence I wouldn't be better. My mother always used to tell me: 'You do write a very good letter, dear.' I *can* be a very good administrator. For example, everything ran smoothly when I handled the British Amateur team in the World Championships in Australia in 1979. ISPA has certainly overcome many of the traditional problems of the game. When the International Squash Rackets Federation or some other body tries to lay down the law to us, they have to be very careful. We now have virtual control of the shop window, the competitive side of the game.

As the game continued to develop at an unprecedented pace, and squash became a commercial success, Barrington was also able to earn large sums of money from sponsorship deals. Fifteen years ago, the SRA was John Horry, his occasional assistant and a tiny office. Today, with spacious open-plan offices in Kensington, it has a staff of fourteen and a 1983 budget in excess of £500,000, of which some £200,000 is sponsorship money. As squash has developed into a sport played by millions, a vast new market for equipment has appeared in its wake. And as the market expanded so have Barrington's earnings as major companies fought for the endorsement of the most famous squash player in the world.

In 1972, Malcolm Hamer became Barrington's agent, and in the eight years from 1973 to 1980, a total of £323,000 of Barrington's squash court earnings passed through Hamer's London office. Hamer recalls that, in 1973, his first full year of looking after Jonah, his earnings off the court were £4,800. Six years later in 1979, his earnings were £75,000. 'The first contract we obtained was with Litesome Sports, the British manufacturer. This ran for three years from March 1973 and although the guarantees were small – he was only paid £1,000 a year – the royalties were four per cent and that is where the money came from. Litesome brought out a complete range of squash clothes all of which bore the Barrington name. They sold a lot of products and he must have earned £20,000 over the first three-year period.'

Later came a far more significant footwear contract with Adidas. Hamer estimates the highly successful Barrington squash shoes earned £47,000 between 1976 and 1979. The shoes had been so successful that Adidas decided to produce an entire Barrington range of squash equipment to satisfy the growing market and on 1 January 1979, a £340,000 contract was signed over seven years with Jonah guaranteed £45,000 for each of the first two years and subsequently £50,000 annually for the remaining five years. Malcolm Hamer firmly believed that this Adidas contract would make Jonah a millionaire: 'We were telling each other we would probably see a million pounds for Jonah Barrington. The rationale was that at the time Adidas were probably the best marketers of sports goods in the world. They had really proved it in the previous three years with the amount of money generated from the footwear contract. But as it turned out, we had negotiated the right contract at the wrong time. If they had gone into production quickly and put the full power of their promotion machine behind Barrington, as they had with the footwear, it would have been a different story. But it wasn't until near the end of the first three-year period that they managed to get some newly designed Barrington squash rackets into the shops. But none of this was Jonah's fault. There were internal company problems between Germany and France. While the Germans effectively held the power, they had no idea what squash was all about and they failed to understand the nature of the squash market.'

Considerable though the amount of money was that Barrington earned off court during his association with Hamer, his agent always believed that Barrington's contract with Ascot should have earned him far more: 'It was a seven-year contract from 1971–8 and the guarantees were something like £1,000 a year going up by six per cent each year. But the royalties should have been a great deal higher. In any squash player's contract, the biggest area should be his rackets. But when I became Jonah's agent he was already committed to this Ascot contract. The firm produced an excellent racket range and I still cannot understand why he only earned about £50,000 in seven years when everywhere I went, not only in this country but abroad, I was forever seeing Ascot rackets with his name on them. Sports companies in my opinion are quite incapable of using sports personalities to boost their sales. They are complete amateurs. They don't promote enough, they don't do enough advertising and when they do in-store promotions, they usually do them badly. If I had been Dunlop I would never have allowed Barrington out of my grip. I would have given him everything he wanted. I would have made everything on the Dunlop squash list by Barrington, and if he had made a million, Dunlop would have made £10 million.'

In June 1980, Barrington and Hamer ended their association. Life with Jonah may have been interesting for Hamer but he was not the easiest person to handle: 'I have a great respect for Jonah and still think of him as a friend. But you are most critical of your friends and I can see him warts and all. I felt he didn't harness his great appeal as well as he might have done. He was obsessed with training to the exclusion of everything else, which is ridiculous. Sometimes he would not turn up to make an after-dinner speech because he would rather play squash. I was always irritated by his turning up late. To my mind it showed a certain contempt for the audience. I once arranged a North American tour for him and he pulled out with an injury just a few days before he was due to leave. At the end of our association he turned up at least an hour late for a clinic. Admittedly it was somewhere near Hull. He complained I hadn't given him the right directions but, as I pointed out, other clients of mine such as Gareth Edwards, Barry John, Gerald Davies and Mick McManus had never complained of being given the wrong directions and they had always arrived on time and in good order. But although I was often sweating, he always kept everybody happy when he did arrive. I remember once, we agreed that he should play two opponents for the best of three at a Staffordshire country club. When we arrived, the owner calmly announced he had got together a Midland Select team and Jonah was going to play all five of them the best of five. "This is nonsense," I said. "Let's leave." But to his eternal credit, Jonah played all five players after we had reduced it to the best of three games.'

'Of course I can be unreliable,' agrees Barrington. 'Of course I do what I want to do because I've always been that way. Of course I don't always arrive on the dot. But I have always arrived on the day! I have never broken an engagement unless I've had a genuine injury and unfortunately in the years I was with Malcolm I did have a terrible injury syndrome. What happened at that Staffordshire club was absolutely typical. People who promoted these evenings were forever saying, "I'm sure you wouldn't mind doing this and that as well, would you?" Malcolm is a decent, civilised man, unlike most agents. We were right for each other for those first few years. But I felt he was getting increasingly less interested in my playing career. I think he felt the game had reached the stage where it was going down a perpetual dry gully and it wasn't going to advance. I badly need to get involved with people who are motivated and I felt we had got into a rut.'

So in June 1980, Barrington terminated his association with Malcolm Hamer together with his contract with Adidas which had earned him £140,000 in three years and, acting on his own behalf, he proceeded to negotiate a new five-year contract with Dunlop.

Unlike many sportsmen, Barrington views sponsorship in utterly idealistic terms. While others may be quite content with a set fee and the odd photographic session, Barrington has never been prepared to take his money and run. He insists on some say in determining the quality of product which will bear his name. The contracts he negotiates place an emphasis on royalties and insist on effective promotions programmes:

I think all the dealings we have had in the sponsorship area have been very disappointing. So many companies have such unwieldy internal organisations. There also seems to be the perennial problem of the retailer being unable to get delivery of what he wants. I remember a Birmingham sports shop owner telling me that the Adidas Gold squash shoe was the best they had ever had. It cost about £24, and although the shop had never been known for footwear, that shoe had sold consistently well. Time and time again people would come up to me and say how good the Barrington Gold was. But Adidas didn't have any confidence it would sell in large quantities. So when they put it in the shops at the beginning of October, it had sold out by the end of the month. And do you know what the next delivery date was? April! After the season had ended.

The concept of the royalty deal is superb providing everybody tries hard. The top Ascot racket was absolutely brilliant. They asked me what features constituted an ideal squash racket and I told them that the ideal racket is about eight ounces with a tiny bit of weight in the head, and a little bit of give in the structure so that it doesn't break like all light rackets do at the moment. Unbelievably, they came up with exactly the racket I wanted using a cane lamination. I gave them my ideas and they produced the goods. That is the way I like it to be. It upsets me if somebody comes up and says this shoe with your name on it is crippling me. That is why Dunlop will, I hope, have the confidence to produce a newly designed range of Barrington shoes because as I don't wear the present Dunlop shoe I honestly don't feel I can endorse it.

But I am glad to be with Dunlop now. They are a British company, I get on well with them and I want to have superb rackets, clothing, and shoe ranges. I was sad in many ways to leave Adidas but Dunlop have already done more promotional work in a few months, including tours abroad, than I ever did with Adidas.

Squash may not have made Barrington a millionaire yet but he has earned what most people would consider a fortune out of the game. In September 1975, the Barringtons bought an attractive Edwardian country house with a stable block and five acres of grounds a mile-and-a-half outside Solihull, the exclusive residential town near Birmingham. There Jonah lives with Madeline and their two sons, Nicholas, eight, named after Jonah's brother, and Jonah Paul, four. Barrington has been careful not to force his sons into the sport – though, at his own request, young Nicholas had his first racket and his first lesson (from Aman) on his eighth birthday. Today the Barrington house is probably worth about £250,000. Barrington may no longer be one of the game's top half-a-dozen players but his public appeal remains. His new contract with Dunlop no doubt will earn him in excess of £50,000 a year and if he averaged just one squash clinic a week, his annual earnings would be beyond the £80,000 mark. So squash has made Barrington a wealthy man but it is no more than he deserves. How many footballers of average talent are earning higher sums without showing anything approaching his dedication? Long after other sportsmen have been forgotten Barrington will be remembered as the man who created the squash boom. As Dicky Rutnagur says: 'All those people who have built courts, made squash rackets and produced squash balls owe Jonah a big debt. If they all wrote a £50,000 cheque for him they would be doing him no kindness, for they owe it to him.'

12. Fit for Life

When Jonah Barrington placed his first hesitant foot on the squash ladder in 1964, specific fitness training for squash was at an embryonic stage and for many of the leading players it was not on their list of priorities. But how things have changed. Today we have reduction training, regenerative training, interval training, ghosting, aerobics, anaerobics, mobility exercises – the list is almost endless. And if you manage all of that, you are highly likely to contract sympathetic overtraining, or even worse, parasympathetic overtraining. This is the jargon of the endurance athlete, the long-distance runner and the Tour de France cyclist. It was Jonah who brought it into squash, having at one time or another experimented with every conceivable type of training:

> Before I arrived, no one trained specifically for squash; it was just a means of keeping fit for other sports such as rugby or soccer. And at the end of every March the squash gear would be stowed away until the following October – even the top players accepted this. Only a couple of the top British players did any sort of background fitness work. Gerald Massey would run in Rotten Row every morning before going to his office in the City and Michael Oddy would take time off work to prepare for a big tournament.
>
> The theory was that squash was just a winter pursuit and that not only was it an unsuitable game for the summer, there was also the grave danger that, if one didn't have a break, one would become stale. One of the reasons why I reached the top so quickly was that I played throughout the summers of 1965 and

1966 and thus got in four seasons instead of two. The only other person I've seen improve so rapidly was Jahangir, and he was in the hands of experts all the time.

Although Jonah may be too polite to mention it, the experts in charge of Jahangir's development all learnt the Barrington methods at first hand before applying them to Jahangir, and in a dog-eat-dog world other players, too, absorbed his hard-won knowledge and used it to their own advantage, engineering his downfall at a time when his own powers were sadly diminishing. But probably the most fundamental reason for Jonah's decline was his selfless and relentless determination, for he had undoubtedly worn parts of his body out, using himself as a guinea-pig while researching training methods up some spectacularly blind alleys:

I remember the Indian SRA secretary, Ahmad Peermohamed, telling me that Hashim Khan used to do a thousand duck waddles a day and so I immediately embarked on duck waddle routines which involve assuming the position of a cossack dancer and bouncing around. I did these for a couple of weeks before a terrible reaction hit me in the knees. I could hardly get up the stairs to the SRA in the morning. John Horry was really worried and sent me to the Middlesex Hospital where I was told that I had been on the verge of crippling myself permanently.

Another blind alley was the raw egg diet that Nasrullah put me on; raw egg beaten up in milk. 'This is very good for you, make you strong', he told me. So, as always if Naz said something, I did it. I had terrible trouble keeping the stuff down but I persevered with it. It was the summer of 1965 and I had been called in to practise with the British team that was going to South Africa. One day I had to leave the court because I felt very dizzy and I remember Richard Boddington carrying me to the changing rooms and stripping off my kit. 'Christ,

166

Jonah, what on earth have you been doing?' he said, because when he saw me stripped off he thought I'd just got out of Belsen, I was so thin.

I told him about the raw egg diet and he and some other members of the team insisted on taking me out for a large steak followed by enormous amounts of ice cream and fruit salad. The basic mistake I'd made, of course, was that Naz had never intended me to eat *just* raw egg in milk, it was supposed to be in addition to my normal diet.

Those were the days before sports medicine became an exact science and athletes' training schedules were not pre-scribed on the basis of cardiovascular efficiency, the level of body fat or oxygen uptake. Consequently Jonah frequently overdid things and there were days when he was barely able to function:

I did far too much too often. Naz never stopped me because his attitude was that, however hard you worked, you could always work harder. He was aware that he had never had such discipline himself after his early phase and he regularly reminded me of this. People used to ask me how I could accept this from a man who was a heavy smoker and who drank quite a lot and was generally out of condition. I explained to them that Nasrullah knew what was required because he had failed himself, he felt he knew where his brother Roshan had failed, and was determined that I should not follow the same path. Consequently he could never have seen it as a problem if I worked too hard. But I *did* work too hard. So much of what I was doing was unprecedented in squash and when I reached my limit an inner voice would always demand that I did it once more.

That inner voice continues to dictate to Jonah for, although it is now accepted that a weekly rest day is beneficial, he will never permit himself such self-indulgence: rest days are for other people and not for Jonah Barrington, for despite overwhelming evidence to the contrary, Barrington, amazingly, considers himself to be an extremely lazy person. Without doubt, his continuing inability to let up for a day, together with the unsuitability of much of his early training, triggered the physical erosion that hit him in his thirties:

> I wasn't training, I was *straining*. I did too many heavy sessions with too little recovery, what I call total reduction sessions. There were too many periods of breaking down rather than building up. I had no remedial runs, no recuperative runs. In fact I can't even remember such a thing as an easy run. I would always have a very long run in the morning, anything up to ten miles – and never less than five – followed by a series of sit-ups, press-ups, trunk-curls and squat-thrusts. Then, during the day, I would have a couple of sessions on court, even though I might be shattered. I'd always force myself through because I was convinced that this would make me psychologically strong. I was in my early twenties, the ideal age for me to absorb such a load. I had a body that could twist and turn and respond to every question I posed.
>
> But in the end I broke down. I had pushed my body beyond the limits of reality, and without doubt the primary cause was the constant thought of playing Geoff Hunt. We now know that suppling and mobility exercises ease much of the strain on joints and ligaments, but I found out too late, and impaired mobility was the price I paid. There was never a thing wrong with me until I was 33 and then suddenly, there I was, absolutely crippled. Everything went wrong: I had trouble with my back, I had an operation on the elbow of my racket arm because it had worn out, and two operations on my right knee. The five years between 35 and 40 were more like fifty years.

One of the main reasons why Barrington and Hunt trained so hard was that for years they had no one to play in practice. When Jonah finally settled in Birmingham in 1971 there was no one in the immediate area capable of taking a point off him; he was so far ahead of the other British players that they tended to avoid him for the sake of their morale. Hunt, living in Melbourne, suffered similarly. Even now Jonah will travel the hundred miles from Birmingham to Heathrow just to practise with the New Zealander, Ross Norman. It is no surprise, therefore, that he tends to be unsympathetic with players who complain that they are out of condition because they have been short of match practice. 'I once gave Bryan Patterson a rollicking after I had slaughtered him in a match in the North of England. I don't think he even scored a point and he claimed lack of practice as an excuse. I told him that anyone can run, skip, do the conditioning exercises, practise on court and simulate the squash movement by ghosting. Having no one to play is no excuse for being out of condition – it's never been an excuse for Hunt and it's never been an excuse for me. Even in the early days I still spent a prodigious amount of time on court. I would practise a single shot for anything up to an hour, whereas other players would practise their entire repertoire of shots and be away in twenty minutes. Nasrullah only had such a wonderful drop shot because he used to spend anything up to three hours practising it, and he would emphasise that it was its sheer repetition that made it second nature in a match.'

Nevertheless, it is easier to groove one's strokes if there is somebody to feed the ball to you and, in Bomber Harris, Jonah has the best in the world. The two men first met in 1971 when, as an RAF physical training instructor, Bomber was training the England badminton squad; and such was his success that they beat a European select side, containing most of the Danish wizards, 6–1 – a success they have rarely enjoyed since he ceased to be responsible for them. Through the grapevine Jonah had heard about the intense training that had wrought such a miracle and, ever-eager to use himself as a guinea-pig, he arranged to take part in one of their sessions. Bomber, now an astonishingly fit fifty-year-old, vividly remembers their first meeting at RAF Innsworth. 'I knew Jonah was the world champion and to me he was a superstar. I was thrilled yet apprehensive. The badminton blokes thought I was the bees' knees, but here was someone who could really tell if I was the bees' knees or not. I was a bit frightened of him at first. He had piercing eyes which always seemed to stare. In those days he had long hair and was very lean and animalistic. He looked just like a champion should look and there was no doubt that he was extremely fit.'

Bomber's badminton boys, although very fit after their regular workouts, were also very apprehensive as they lined up for the opening sprints with this newcomer who looked every inch the fittest man in the world. It would have amazed them to know that Jonah was equally apprehensive. But worse was to come for as he surged into his first length of the aircraft hangar, which served as a gym, he tweaked a hamstring.

Bomber remembers: 'We started off with 60-yard bursts backwards and forwards as a warm-up and I thought "Christ, he's pulled". With his pride at stake, Jonah was under pressure from the word go but he carried on and it eased out after about ten minutes. It was one hell of a session and went on right throughout the afternoon: half-an-hour's running, followed up with a three-mile road run with a medicine ball, and then three circuits over 25 air-raid shelters, each one 12 foot high and covered in grass; finally some circuit training before we finished off with a game of volleyball. Jonah loved it – he told us that it was the best training he had ever had, and he came back again and again. One point I noticed in particular was that, during a session, as the others flagged, he seemed to get stronger. I was impressed by his tremendous drive and competitiveness. He *had* to be one of the best: he stood out. Now while my lads had done a lot of this type of training, Jonah hadn't, but he handled it tremendously well. A lesser man would have caved in after half-an-hour.'

The respect was mutual and, in 1974, following his defeat by Mo Yasin in the British Open, Jonah made contact again with Bomber Harris. Analysing his defeat, Jonah realised that he was not spending enough time on court. Would Bomber take him full time? Bomber, who had recently left the RAF, jumped at the chance: 'I've always said that the greatest thing to happen to me was being given the opportunity to work with Jonah. He is a great professional, a champion, in every sense of the word. I felt very privileged because, at that time, I couldn't even play squash, so for two years I just took him for fitness work.'

Bomber's régime began with remorseless two-hour fitness sessions, sessions now considered by Jonah to have been the hardest training of his career. His first experience of what was to follow came on the morning of 30 June 1974, at the West Warwicks squash club. Determined to accomplish all that his new trainer asked of him, and more, Jonah did 78 press-ups in a single minute followed by 52 sit-ups also in a minute flat. But even more remarkable to Bomber was that on a subsequent circuit with a medicine ball, Jonah repeated the majority of the exercises, achieving even more repetitions the second time around.

But it was all very well for the two fanatics to achieve such incredible results. This was merely a means to the all-important end, but, gradually, news of Jonah's remarkable feats of fitness began to spread.

One morning, Bomber and I drove up to the club and, as we rounded the corner, there was this enormous banner declaring 'Welcome to the Rollocks'. Now at first glance, both Bomber and I were convinced that it said something else and we each looked at the other and started laughing. But when we got inside, we learned that the Rollocks were a Dutch hockey club who were over for the weekend. Anyway, we started to train and a few Rollocks began to appear in the gallery, which set us off laughing again, and within a few minutes there were 25 or 30 of them up there. By this time, I was engrossed in the session and had done about five minutes with the medicine ball, going forward and back, throwing it to Bomber. When I finished, there was a round of applause from the Rollocks, whose numbers had swollen The gallery was packed with Dutch hockey players and their supporters. For the next twenty minutes, they clapped everything I did and I loved it.

I was now getting really motivated and so was Bomber who was driving me on relentlessly. We had an audience and, what's more, they were in the palm of our hand. Then, all of a sudden, they quietly filed out and I realised that they had gone off to play their hockey matches. But some 70 minutes later, they came back. By this time, I had been going for an hour and three-quarters. One Rollock poked his head over the top of the gallery and, within a minute, there were soon 50 Rollocks up there.

They just couldn't believe I was still there – there was absolute silence. I was now in the most intensive stage when we do about 15 one-minute exercises, squat-thrusts, ghosting, jumping up the wall, and so on. When I finally finished there was thunderous applause, but I couldn't do any encores. It had been a particularly ruthless session and when I reached home I couldn't take anything in except flat coke until about midnight.

I did about four such sessions a week, which was possibly too much. Two would have been better but both of us were suckers for punishment and we were restricted to fitness work because Bomber hadn't then acquired the skills he now has with the racket.

Over the years Jonah has been host to many of the world's top players, most of whom have attempted to keep up with his training only to fold after a couple of days. One year the South African Ian Holding visited Britain well before the start of the British Amateur to train with Jonah: it was very nearly the end of him. Holding was in his early twenties and Barrington in his mid thirties, but despite the obvious advantages of age, it still took the young South African two weeks to recover from his ordeal. Up against nearly twenty years of background training, it is not entirely surprising that many of the younger players are unable to absorb anything like Jonah's schedule. 'But he has always had to work bloody hard,' says Bomber. 'We did thousands of different sessions but whenever I slipped one in that he'd not done before he'd zoom through it as if it were a warm-up. I could also tell by the increasing number of repetitions how his co-ordination was improving. He was awkward at first in jumping over the medicine ball from side to side, but with his hard work he improved so much that he could do 160 or 170 bounces over the ball in a minute-and-a-half. This is horrific continuous leg work. What I find really amazing is that despite his fitness he didn't get a just reward for all that work – he wasn't winning tournaments. Perhaps his opponents knew that they had to work harder than they had before and once he had lost it it was as though a cloud had been lifted; everybody took heart. But Jonah had led the way and shown them just how hard they would have to work if they were to beat him. Our type of training kept him superbly fit, but there was no one really for him to play. How he kept his skills intact, I'll never know. All he could do was to go on court by himself and practise for hour upon hour. Even in the British squads that I've taken no player would do that; he'd complain of being bored after twenty minutes.'

In 1981 Jonah underwent two operations on his badly worn knee. For the majority of athletes, such surgery would have signalled the end of the road; but Jonah Barrington stared defeat in the eye and defied it. The following nine months saw a constant battle for fitness with Jonah exercising on a canoe ergometer at Birmingham University. Despite his resolution, there were many times when he thought he would never play again. Thus, every visit to the court is now a doubly enjoyable experience for him, an unexpected bonus. Not for nothing has he distilled twenty years of gruelling training into an exact science: every scrap of knowledge he has acquired is now marshalled to keep him going for another twenty, every lesson learned through bitter experience.

Warming up is one of his strongest creeds and today he even has a warm-up to prepare for his warm-up!

I wish I had realised the importance of warming up far sooner than I did. I am confident that I could have regained my Open title in 1975, but the lack of a proper warm-up cost me the quarter-final against

Gogi Alauddin. I had not played an enormous amount of competition that year, and the night I played Gogi we were to be the last match on, with Jahan and Mohibullah before us. I remember they played a monstrous match; it lasted for about an hour and three-quarters.

It looked as though Mohi was going to win in straight games so at the end of the second I went away for my warm-up outside, which was stupid of me really, because it was freezing out there. But I managed to get warmed up and came in to find they were in a cliffhanger of a third game which Hiddy won. They went on to the fourth game which was very long and drawn out so I went out to warm up again and came back to find that Jahan had levelled and they were to play a fifth game. So I warmed up yet again and when they finally finished, and Gogi and I were knocking up, I knew that something was wrong because I felt like a boiled lobster. What had happened was that the crowd had been in there for about three hours, the television lights were on, the temperature had risen enormously and I felt I was playing somewhere in the tropics. It's hardly surprising I was terribly lethargic.

Clearly I'd warmed up *too* much and, feeling very nervy as well, I never really came to terms with him; he beat me in straight games. I made the kind of critical errors in the third that I would never otherwise have made, and I was out. At no time did I feel any sense of sparkiness. After that I knew I would have to prepare for a repeat of those conditions and had to do some pretty heavy thinking with regards to warming up. How many warm-ups could I do? I believe that the heart should be well worked in order to get what is still called your second wind. That's why I've always turned the heat up during training and pressured myself. Alright, I've done some daft things as regards pressure, but I've used the heat thing over the years because I've discovered that the top player must be accustomed to playing in heat and humidity.

The ultimate test is in somewhere like Singapore where, even having trained assiduously for three months for a particular event, you find that after a couple of minutes of running hither and thither you're reduced to a long dribble of sweat. In 1979 I went out to Singapore two weeks before the tournament began so I could acclimatise, and that's when I had my best win for a number of years over Mohibullah. The humidity out there is appalling. After very little time it is impossible to get forward or to perform a quick movement and the interval between games is really worse than continuing to play; the break provides no relief whatever, it merely allows you to dwell on just how awful you feel.

But the worst humidity I ever encountered was in Karachi in 1976. I was playing in their new complex which at the time had just been completed but was not air-conditioned. Geoff Hunt told me he thought I'd enjoy playing Mohibullah there because my game would have him in difficulty, with the long rallying and steady play, and he thought I might get to Mohi mentally.

We duly played in front of the President of Pakistan, the late Ali Bhutto. The first point was long and got the blood flowing through the veins and the old ticker pumping. It was ideal and Hunt was up there in the front row giving me the thumbs-up as if to assure me I was going about things the right way.

It was a smashing opening rally and must have lasted about two and a half minutes and it was just the job – but suddenly I found myself completely paralysed. I just felt terribly ill, and five minutes later I felt even worse. I lasted about 35 minutes and got about seven points. The worst part was between games when we went outside for air. There wasn't a breath of wind and it was just as humid. To make matters worse, a plague of mosquitos were waiting to get at us.

Despite all his injuries, and the fact that his tournament programme has been drastically reduced. Jonah remains determined to extract the maximum from his physical resources. His programme may not be as heavy as it once was but it is still formidable. 'On Tuesdays and Thursdays I train with Bomber for an hour-and-a- quarter in the morning and then in the afternoon I'll play whoever happens to be in town or practise on my own. My sessions with Bomber are pressure training and I'll have all the gear on – two tops and tracksuit bottoms, with the heating turned on full blast. On the days that I'm not with Bomber I run for about forty- five minutes, do stomach exercises and weights and play in the afternoon.'

All this effort is achieved on a surprisingly small amount of food. Jonah finds it impossible to eat before his morning run – a croissant and a cup of tea stand a very good chance of reappearing, even if consumed two hours before he sets out. Madeline rustles up a very tasty line in snacks for the inevitable lunchtime visitors but Jonah will sit supping a cup of his favourite Earl Grey tea and nibbling miserly at a couple of biscuits. Experience has proved that if he eats any more before his afternoon game the fate of the morning croissant would be repeated. Madeline does manage to get a meal into him later at night but it is rarely until about 9 o'clock that he is sufficiently recovered from his day's training to eat with any relish. Amazingly enough, 'Jonah does not have a naturally strong constitution,' says Madeline. 'He's had to work hard for every ounce of his fitness, and it breaks down very quickly. He gets boils in his ears, ulcers in his mouth and he suffers from piles. He's peed blood on and off for years. It's all stress!'

According to Azam Khan, who considers Barrington's training methods far from advisable, all this is avoidable: 'His training method silly. Wasting time. Only thing is get in that court and hit, hit, hit. Play hard game against somebody better than you. When I was world champion, I couldn't run for bus, get stitches. Brother Hashim, he never do any training. Before I come over here for Open I never play squash all summer, maybe tennis sometimes, just before squash season start playing. Players fitter now but no good with the stroke. The standard is not at all with the stroke. Play somebody every day better than you for as long as you can stand it. Practise your weak shot, stand there and hit, hit, hit – you soon get it.' But, as Jonah would say, 'That *is* training, Azam', and he never had anyone to play.

Today, even though he has partially withdrawn from competitive squash, Barrington continues to push himself remorselessly, maintaining a level of fitness that for the rest of us will remain as much a mystery as the view from the top of Everest. His reasoning is based on his insistence that his income must derive from his ability as a squash player, not from his status as a celebrity. He has chosen a hard road but he is as fundamentally ascetic now as he was when he was 26, and there is an inevitability about his uncompromising attitude. As he explains: 'I went to Stockholm recently and they produced their best Under-19-year-old to play me at the end of a clinic. Obviously while giving the clinic, I hadn't had any opportunity to warm up but he was bouncing away and raring to go – and he was bloody good. I played him the best of three and I killed him in the end. But I tell you what, he could have won 2–0. At the end of the second game, the promoter came and said we'd better make it the best of three because the boy was starting to get tired. I'm glad he did because I was on the rack in the first game and a half, trying to get going, while he was playing out of his mind. So I still have to do all this training, otherwise I might get beaten after my clinics in my exhibition games. Some people don't understand that spectators generally enjoy my clinics but they're really waiting to see me play – and play well. It's not my job to let them down.'

Just how much work Barrington does now he is no longer on the professional circuit can be gauged by looking at a week in his diary for February 1983:

Saturday Sunday Feb 12 and 13 Coach national squad for two days at Leek Wootton club. Both days, run four miles first thing in the morning in garden. Train with Moussa Helal, Egyptian professional, on Saturday and session with Bomber on Sunday. Play all 16 kids on the first day – started to fade a bit as played Moussa beforehand.

Monday Feb 14 9.30–11am. Run four miles round garden followed by session on exercise bike, abdominal exercises and skipping. 11 am–2 pm interview for book. Then on court at Albany Hotel with Mo Asran, followed by more abdominal and quad exercise in the hotel gym. Session lasts from 3–5.

Tuesday Feb 15 Play Mo Asran at Albany again with exercises afterwards – 11 to 12.45. 5.00 pm. Run 20 laps around garden followed by 300 abdominal exercises without break.

Wednesday Feb 16 Five hours' sleep. Up 6.30 am to catch plane from Birmingham to Gatwick and then fly to Stockholm. Gave clinic and exhibition in evening for 3 hrs. Bed at 2 am after midnight meal.

Thursday Feb 17 Six hours' sleep. Then run 4 miles on forest track near Olympic Stadium. Temperature –7°. Long time to warm up, chugged along as best I could on the solid snow surface. Did 240 abdominals in snow afterwards – real penance. Shower and then taken to club where I was working that night. 12.30–1.30 pm. Court practice on my own followed by newspaper interview. 3 hr clinic and exhibition in evening where they produce best Under-19-year-old in Sweden. Late dinner, 5 hrs' sleep.

Friday Feb 18 Woke 6.30 to catch early plane to Heathrow. Fly Heathrow to Birmingham. Midday – running four miles round garden in track suit with wet suit over the top in a lethargic stupor. Do my abdominals then Madeline drives me to Ipswich. 7.30–10.50 pm. Clinic at Martleşham Health club. Play David Taylor, Suffolk No 1. Go to sleep at hotel at about 2.30 am absolutely drained.

This then is the reason that Barrington continues to drive himself so hard in training. With a diary like this, he has to, simply to survive.

13. The Master Takes Charge

After twenty years in the public eye, the world's most famous squash player has no desire to retire. Jonah Barrington intends to continue playing and training because, as he admits, life would be unbearable if he couldn't. But with an eye to the future, he has found a new challenge to establish himself as the world's greatest coach. In 1982, he was appointed the Squash Racket Association's National Squad Coach with a brief to break the dominance of Pakistan and Australia and to make England the strongest squash-playing country in the world.

'We have hung our whole élite development structure on Jonah,' says Bob Morris, the SRA's chief executive. 'We have made a conscious decision that he is the man who can produce the goods. He will have a major, if not total say, in shaping the development of our élite young players even though, to be frank, there are those who disagree with the appointment. They argue that Jonah lacks formal coaching qualifications, and they don't feel he is the right person for this role. They think his creed in squash is simply fitness and tightness. But we are aware that he has changed quite radically in recent years and that he is now varied in his play. It is quite clear to us that he doesn't want negative play to be the basis of his coaching and he has already proved his great ability as a coach and motivator. In 1979, when he was put in charge of the British Amateur team for the World Championships in Australia, no one thought they would win the championships. But they did and Jonah was the man who inspired them. He is also marvellous with youngsters – you only have to watch his weekend sessions to see this. At the moment we are looking for a major sponsor to support the whole coaching system with Jonah handling the top juniors and our best senior players. But until we achieve that sponsorship, we are forced to rely heavily on Jonah's enormously generous goodwill and his utter dedication to the furtherance of squash in this country.'

Since 1978, in fact, Barrington has been working with some of the country's best juniors in a scheme instigated by a friend of his, Edward Poore, an Old Harrovian and dedicated squash enthusiast who organised 'Jonah Barrington Weekends', from which the national junior squad system has developed. And it has developed to such an extent that there are now Under-19, Under-16, Under-14, Under-12 and even Under-10 squads. 'Nobody, with the possible exception of the Royal Ballet, has ever done anything like this,' says Jonah proudly.

There are nine area coaches reporting to SRA Central Administrator, John Taylor, and keeping an eye open for talented youngsters. In addition Jonah has enlisted the help of Bomber Harris, Vivian Grisogono, a leading physiotherapist with experience at international athletics level, and Dr Craig Sharp, a member of the British Olympic medical committee and Lecturer in Exercise Physiology at Birmingham University.

Barrington's attitude to coaching is as refreshing as it is thorough and his detractors will be disappointed to know that he believes his own training schedules to be wildly unsuitable for youngsters whose bodies are not totally developed:

I don't believe that until a certain age there is any point in giving individual training programmes. But I do believe that the kids must be made aware of the meaning of the word training and learn that it is something that will become increasingly important as they get older. But at the moment, I do not want the boys involved in training activities or repetitive exercises. Even when the right time comes, what is good for one may not necessarily be right for the other.

I have brought in Viv Grisogono to advise the boys on suppling exercises, protective exercises for the knees and back and, for those who play rugby, the neck. We try to ensure they avoid injuries in other sports once we have found out what they are up to. Craig Sharp attends every squad session to test for specific aspects of fitness such as vital capacity, speed, strength and endurance. We also continually monitor body fat.

We are a general advisory service for the boys and we try to get them into good habits, but at the same time we allow their natural expression to manifest itself. If a kid has the wrong grip, we would encourage him to change it for his own good. That is one of the reasons why it is so essential to get them as early as eight or nine years old.

Barrington has a quick response for those ludicrous enough to point out that he has no formal coaching qualifications. He argues that the advice given in the majority of the coaching manuals bears no relation to the way in which the game is played at the highest level:

There always has to be a great dividing line between orthodox and unorthodox, continual argument about right and wrong footwork. The original creators of the 'great guidelines' have given the game a coaching divinity which scarcely relates to the way it is played at the highest level. For instance, we have all been assured at one time or another that we must 'go to the T' after we serve. But that's rubbish. It does happen from time to time, but there isn't a player at any level who doesn't feel a damn sight less exposed if he lays back a bit behind the T area.

I say the coaching manual is sterile because so many sports need improvisation, and this is especially so in squash where one is forced into situations where one has to hit the ball off either one leg or the other. But the coaching manual talks about hitting the ball off the correct foot, the correct leg, getting your feet right – this is the way it *must* be done. I've looked at the great exponents of the game during my career, and of course there have been common denominators, but many of these common denominators are simply not in the manual.

181

I greatly admired the coaching strip Bjorn Borg did in the *Daily Express,* which started off with the fundamentals – getting the ball over the net – and preferably over the lower part of the net. Why go over the high part of the net when it is easier to hit it over the low part of the net? No, it's not as simple as that, of course, but it's great to see somebody with more enterprise in his approach to coaching.

I would love to be recognised as the world's greatest coach and I'm confident that when it comes to dealing with the older kids, let's say those over the age of fifteen, I know a damn sight more about the subject than anyone else. I know more about the preparation for the game and the winding down afterwards as well – that's all born of years of practice and experience and not mere theory. I also know that I motivate people better than anyone else – nearly twenty years on a daily basis makes that area a no- contest! Perhaps I may not yet be the best coach when it comes to dealing with sheer technique with the really young kids – that's another facet of expertise I will have to gain – but my strength is as a motivating force, as an example if you like – being there, guiding them, overseeing the other coaches and then taking them through from the critical ages of 15, 16 and 17, from the junior to senior levels, and, with the benefit of my experience, helping them to cope with all the mental and physical pressures that they will meet along the way.

The main reason why Jonah is himself still functioning at a frighteningly efficient level is that he has always been careful with himself after the rigours of training and competition. 'Jonah has looked after himself tremendously well,' says Dr Craig Sharp, his friend and medical adviser since 1969. 'He's always had lots of sleep and if he has a late night he'll lie in in the morning to compensate. He makes sure he has plenty of rest and warmth and since Madeline has been looking after him he has eaten well. He has lots of warm baths and he's been very lucky in never having had a major debilitating illness such as glandular fever or bad bronchitis. And his body is marvellously suited for squash. He has exactly the right combination of fast and slow muscle and can function efficiently in oxygen debts that would be intolerable for other people. Much of this he has achieved through training, but nature gave him the ideal equipment on which to work and he still works extremely hard. His body fat level is still only seven per cent and to maintain that at his age he must subject himself to a terrifyingly disciplined régime.'

Research has shown that during exercise natural morphines are released into the blood. This accounts for the fact that so many people experience a feeling of wellbeing after strenuous exercise. This is one reason why it's almost impossible today to walk down the street after dark without being cannoned into by a succession of joggers, all seeking their fix of natural morphine – a condition also known as the 'joggers' high'. Could Jonah be hooked on training? Is he an exercise junkie? Dr Sharp believes that he may well be and tells an alarming story to illustrate what happens to people who stop training suddenly after years of effort. 'In the 1950s there was a Scottish international runner who stopped training and competing when he got married even though he was at an age where he could have continued. Not long after he stopped running he was admitted to Glasgow Infirmary with an hysterical paralysis of the legs. He was suffering from acute withdrawal symptoms and was advised for the sake of his health to start training again, and quickly.'

There is little likelihood of this happening to Jonah as he has no intention of giving up his training or playing. 'Madeline has been a great motivation to me and she actually got me going again in the 70s when I was beginning to flag, but now she is very determined that I should become involved in other areas. I've said to her a couple of times in quite an angry fashion, "Don't you realise I don't want to give endless after-dinner speeches?" Other people would say that I was cuckoo for turning down a fat fee for giving an after-dinner speech. But I don't want to be with people who are going to gas me with cigar smoke. I don't want to be told that I have a Celtic ability to be entertaining. If I ever thought that was going to be my bread-and-butter I would find it grotesque. I'll do it on occasions provided my bread-and-butter comes from my expertise on the squash court, because the one way I want to express myself is through playing, and I know how much people love to see me play.'

After an enforced lay-off with his knee injury in 1981, Jonah returned to competition in 1982 having doubted for a long time whether he would ever play again. And after winning the British Over-35 title, beating John Easter, he reached the final of the first World Grand Masters Championship. Restricted to players over 35, Jonah was largely responsible for its inception so that he and his contemporaries would have something in which to compete. More than 1,500 people crowded into the National Exhibition Centre in Birmingham but all they saw was the sad sight of Barrington being beaten 3–0 by the 35-year-old Egyptian Ahmed Safwat. Unable to stage one of his famous recoveries, Jonah walked around the court between points with the lame stride of an old man.

Jonah was suffering from one of his occasional attacks of paroxysmal tachycardia, the symptoms of which are a doubling of the heartbeat, an inability to breathe, dizziness and the staggers. A disturbing sight but, as Dr Craig Sharp points out, 'It is serious to Jonah if it happens in a match but there is nothing dangerous about the condition.' The route to recovery is to stop moving, which of course is impossible in the middle of the game. So he had to wait for the break before he could try to relax the tightness in his chest.

For Madeline that match was a terrible experience: 'It was so bad. I didn't even want to go, it drains me to such an extent now that I could flee quite happily in the other direction rather than have the agony of watching him play.' At the dinner that evening after the World Open final between Jahangir Khan and the Australian Dean Williams, Madeline asked Geoff Hunt what it was like not being able to play squash any more: 'It was a hell of a shock to me when he said he didn't really want to play any more. He said he really enjoyed being at home at night and being able to spend time with his children.'

More than ever before, Jonah now plays squash for fun, training to keep really fit for his clinics and exhibitions, and often beating many of the world's best players in practice matches. But when he decides to compete, as he did at the NEC, it can hardly be described as fun, as Madeline well knows:

> Before competition he literally goes to pieces. He can't sleep, he can't eat, and he's irritable to an unbelievable degree. He has a go at the kids, I can't do anything right, and he gets dreadfully depressed. During these periods he's like a dead weight.
>
> He can still play squash in exhibitions and he's terrific in his clinics. I think people get far better value from Jonah in those areas than they do by watching him sweating and struggling so nervously in competition. Now, tired as he is, he will still go for days without sleep prior to an event. He gets to sleep occasionally but not before about five in the morning, so by the time the rest of the family are up we have to creep around so that he can wake up naturally. If anyone wakes him up all hell breaks loose.

Madeline is one of the few people to whom Jonah will listen on the subject of his playing career. To those well-meaning people who advise him to retire in order to preserve his legend his response is simple: 'If I'd listened to those sort of people in the beginning, I'd never have started out.' And he doesn't feel that he is alone in experiencing pre-competitive tension. 'People always assumed that Colin Cowdrey was always very calm, but he has spoken openly about occasions when, driving to the ground, he became so scared that he would actually drive away again. Sportsmen and women literally burn themselves out because they are so frightened of being regarded as idiots. You cannot imagine the hundreds of athletes who have thought of excuses on the day of battle. We actually create reasons for not going. For example, before the final of the 1972 British Open against

Hunt I was desperately hoping that it would snow and the roads would be blocked, because I felt like a person going to the gallows. But there was no alternative, I *had* to go to the gallows.'

'Even in my worst days,' says Madeline, 'when I felt nervous about competing on the track, I never felt like that – I knew I'd have to run and that I'd just have to get on with it. But Jonah said he wasn't going to that 1972 Open, he wasn't going to play. I had no idea what sort of excuse we would have to dream up for all those people, but somehow I got him in the car. On the way over to Abbeydale I fully expected him to tell me to turn the car around and go back. But I kept cajoling him and telling him that even if he wasn't going to play we still had to be there. Of course once we'd arrived he played brilliantly and won, but afterwards I thought, Hell, if I've got to go through this sort of pressure every time, and I'm not even competing, will I be able to take it, will I be able to live with it?'

Because he has had to endure many such agonies, fighting the little voice that reminds us all at times that it is easier to quit than soldier on, Jonah has never had time for athletes who are not, in the best sense of the word, professional in their approach. Displeased by the antics of the team he captained on the disastrous tour of Australia in 1967, he gave an interview to ITV's Brian Moore in which he accused the team of being a bunch of dilettantes and criticised the attitude of the SRA as amateurish:

The SRA rang Brian Moore asking for a copy of the tape because they wanted to decide whether they were going to take action against me, but he told them that the tape had been destroyed in a fire! I believed, and still believe, that so many people in the hierarchy of the SRA were content to see the game remain in the exclusive arena of London's clubland. I didn't like the way that the popular press always seemed to be excluded from any event organised by the SRA. Their defence was that the popular press were always looking for angles and the SRA didn't like angles. To them, the fundamentally important part of the evening was the socialising afterwards. I am no killjoy, and I happily accept that, for large numbers of players, the social aspect of squash is most important. But I'm afraid that, at the highest level of any sport, there isn't all that much room for bags of fun.

The British team in 1967 were incompetent in their approach. They were representing their country and I found their attitude to that was unbelievable. Perhaps part of the overall problem lay in the fact that I was too inexperienced to be in charge. I had little inclination to know what made other people tick. I have always held that when representing one's country you should give 110 per cent. It was always the overriding motivation for me and I felt enormous satisfaction and accomplishment when the team that I coached in 1979 won the World championship in Australia.

There is one spectacle that is certain to have Jonah glazing over and in danger of hurling a shoe through the television screen, and that is the sight of overweight darts and snooker players swilling pints of beer and smoking themselves to death in public while earning enormous sums of money. 'People who purport to be international stars should, in my opinion, look like they fit the bill.'

An uncompromising attitude perhaps, but Jonah would not have achieved what he has without it. He has had to dull his appetites in order to succeed and for long periods of his life he deliberately blotted out the memories of his roistering days in the bars of Dublin lest he succumb once again to such temptations. Nevertheless he is known to enjoy an occasional glass of cider, and Madeline, worried that her husband's puritanical stance will continue until he is carried away in a box, sometimes pours him a glass of a particularly revolting liqueur made up basically of coffee and whisky as a night cap. This Jonah sips happily – perhaps blissfully unaware that it contains any kind of alcohol. 'I know that drink, if taken sensibly, doesn't do any harm, but with me it is much more psychological than anything else, as I have an in-built guilt complex which stems from the time I didn't drink when I was with Nasrullah. But I still believe that if I can discipline myself, I'm more likely to be able to produce what I want to do in my forties. I must maintain my standards of discipline without actually reverting to being a monk again.'

Most people are congenitally unable to change their character after having passed through their formative years and it is one of Jonah's more impressive achievements that he managed to do so. It was not as if he was unaware of what having a good time was. But with the sacrifices have come the rewards and in 1969 his efforts to promote the game of squash and become its finest player were officially recognised when he was awarded the MBE.

In 1969 I had lost in the World Amateur final to Hunt, I'd lost to Nancarrow in the Open, and I'd turned professional in a terrible state of distress. Then, out of the blue, I was awarded the MBE. It was all rather ironic. I was actually in Rhodesia when I was told. I think it was on the recommendation of the ex-England football manager, Walter Winterbottom, who was on the Sports Council and played squash at the Lansdowne. He was very interested in what I was doing and knew the work I'd put in. I felt very honoured but quite astounded.

I was away in South Africa for five or six months after that and it was two years before I went to collect the award. The Palace had been getting quite disturbed and a man used to ring my mother quite regularly wanting to know when I was coming to collect it. He would always ask her about the weather in Cornwall and they would have very pleasant chats. He'd tell her that he understood I was a jolly busy fellow but would I be good enough to come along just so they could keep their paperwork straight? So, in the end, I went.

Nicholas and Nasrullah were my guests and I went along in the full finery with my top hat etc. Inside the Palace I was put in a separate area with the people who were receiving the MBE in my class and while I was under 30 the average age was about 60. The majority of them were pretty venerable and utterly respectable and there I was with my hair down to my trousers; it was quite obvious that I was the nigger in the woodpile. It was assumed I was some sort of pop star. There were no announcements and no one knew who was getting what or why.

As the queue shuffled forward, a small orchestra was playing polite background music. I was looking up at all the magnificent paintings and the ornate plasterwork in this huge room, thinking how glad I was not to have their heating bills, when I was suddenly called forward. The Queen was personally performing the investiture and we were instructed that we had to advance from her right, bow and go forward to collect the award.

As I went in, I caught sight of a couple of elderly dowagers hogging the front row of the stalls directly in front of Nick and Nasrullah. As I advanced on the Queen, one old lady turned to the other and said loudly: 'Good God. It's Geronimo.' Undaunted, I approached the Queen and bowed. Some flunky whispered in her ear, 'Squash player, Your Majesty', and she said politely: 'Do you still play?' She didn't have a clue, poor lady, didn't have a clue . . . do you still play?! I think I muttered something about the fact that in the terms of my sport I was still a relative child, and that was that. I was slightly disappointed by the whole thing. Obviously it wasn't the Queen's fault because after all she can't be expected to know everything, but she could have got some clued-up advisers.

It could be said that the efforts which led to Jonah being awarded the MBE also led directly to the squash boom of the late '60s and early '70s, which only began to lose its momentum when the recession first began to bite in the late '70s. Jonah lays much of the blame, however, firmly at the door of 'the get-rich-quick merchants who thought they were on to a good thing. It's a good job a lot of those people went bust and got their fingers burned – the game is better off without them. What we want in squash are dedicated enthusiasts, not the absentee entrepreneurs that we have had in the past.'

Barrington is fully aware that if the game is to have an even greater impact, then it must inveigle itself onto the nation's television screens. Its failure to do so to date has left him perplexed and bewildered, for he cannot understand why the BBC and the commercial television companies apparently don't share his view that squash is the most compelling and exciting sport ever devised. Apart from the difficulties in seeing the ball, which travels around at a bewildering speed to an eye unaccustomed to its line of flight and the geometry of the court, there is another cruelly paradoxical reason for television's lack of interest. 'The trouble with squash as a televised sport,' says Gary Newbon, Head of Sport for Central Television, 'is that apart from not being able to see the ball clearly, the better the players are the easier they make it look. We can record two top players on a conventional court, but when we show the tape, they look like two old men out for a stroll.'

Another problem is that the television camera shortens distance. But the SRA believes it has found the answer to the technical problems, and Jonah agrees with them. With the introduction of the three- and four-walled transparent courts seen recently at Chichester, Leicester and at the National Exhibition Centre in Birmingham, where a record crowd of more than 1,500 watched a game of squash at the Audi 1982 World Championships, it is possible to shoot through the front and side walls and thus take the viewer into the court and amongst the action.

'A programme we commissioned at Leicester proved that squash *can* work on television *and* be an exciting spectacle,' says SRA secretary Bob Morris. 'And with these courts, I believe that within three years there will be a squash event at the Albert Hall that will be watched by 5,000 or 6,000 people. If television puts enough effort into squash, there could be an enormous interest, although, having said that, I don't feel the British public are going to be terribly interested in watching two Pakistanis playing each other. If we could get some nationalistic feeling going, this could spark

190

off another boom and, for that reason, we will be running a five-a-side series of Test Matches against Pakistan and Australia, hopefully later in 1983. We might not yet have a Number One capable of challenging Jahangir for the top spot but put up a team of five and we measure up pretty well against those two countries.'

Television interest is certainly not dead, for Channel 4 has expressed its willingness to televise a Test Match series, and TVS is working hard on ways to improve and enhance coverage. In Barrington's view, Britain could experience another squash boom that would make what happened in the 1970s look like a minor event. But television plus the success of his coaching programmes is vital to ensure the fulfilment of this vision. Television companies may prefer to choose other sports – after all, why bother with squash and its technical problems when other sports without any major difficulties can be covered – but he believes that once the television camera is taught how to show what is really happening on the squash court – the pain on the players' faces, the varied problems they face and the blood and guts that are part of major contests – squash will become compulsive viewing. But whatever happens, Jonah Barrington's place in the history of the game is already assured. Universally acknowledged as the most effective force for change that squash has ever known, it was he who rang the changes almost single-handedly and it was his powerful personality and determination that swept the sport along on a tidal wave of enthusiasm. Unquestionably, he is the greatest player Britain has ever produced. Six times winner of the coveted British Open, he never failed to reach the quarter-finals of squash's premier championship in fourteen consecutive years. Not unnaturally Jonah rates himself on rather a higher plane. 'Because of my disadvantages, I think I'm the greatest player of all time. If I'd started at the age when Hunt started playing the game I might have won 20 British Opens.'

As is always the case with Jonah, truth is mingled with the absurd. He was disadvantaged compared to the other great players. He did not possess the same level of hand–eye co-ordination, he was short-sighted, and he did not play the game seriously until relatively late in life. He was not as naturally quick as Hashim Khan or Geoff Hunt. But he had the intelligence to realise his shortcomings and do something about them. And it was this brain above all else that enabled him to beat the more naturally gifted players. He would work out what would hurt his opponents most and he would go on doing it to them for hour after hour if necessary. For most of his opponents it was too great a burden to carry around on the court.

The record book says that Geoff Hunt was the greatest player of all time with his eight British Opens, then Hashim Khan with seven, followed by Jonah with six. Some players believe that Hashim was the greatest player of all time because he did not win the British Open until he was 35 years old and was 42 when he won it for the seventh time. Other experts, including Geoff Hunt, think that the Khans would not have been able to operate at their advanced age in today's frenetic, fly-around-the-world, tournament scene. 'Standards in all sports have risen,' explained Geoff, 'and I can't believe that the standard in squash has not improved too. The Khans were never as fit as Jonah or myself, they didn't play so often and the only time Hashim or Azam had a tough game was when they played each other. There certainly wasn't the strength in depth that there is now.'

Geoff may well be right and what rational man would argue with the eight times winner of the British Open? But what he didn't say was that after Jonah had become the world champion, Azam Khan, who provides the bridge between the Khan generations, was still able to take Jonah apart in practise. If pressed, Azam drops hints that he may have been 'carrying' Hashim in at least two of their British Open finals, so if we accept that Azam could have won two of Hashim's titles, and add them to the four he won himself, we arrive at a total of six – the same as Jonah. Azam then calmly announces that he would have won all of Jonah's titles as well!

'You work it out,' he says. 'I retire in '62 season and he come in '67 season. I beat him easy then. He try hard to beat me when he won Australian Amateur in 1968 season.

He came here wearing long track suit, I was laughing at him. I say what's this, Jonah, you going to play in track suit? I was joking with him and I say I'm going to take this off you, you watch it. He went on court in it, very hot club here. I make him work, he soon boiling, take off track suit. Every time after that he come here, make joke of it, he say "Azam, I'm going to beat you today" – he never did.'

Jonah says that Azam was the best player he ever met, though Geoff Hunt was the best player he ever met in competition. Jahangir, in his opinion, has a better all-round game than Hunt, especially in the front of the court, but 'if Jahangir lives until he's 150 he will never have the mind of Hunt, who had the most astonishing ability to maintain his senses under pressure. But when people have asked me about Azam I've always said *he* was the master, and if you could say that any world champion was ever also an apprentice, then I was. I still think that in 1966 Azam was the best player in the world, although there is a world of difference between practice games and competition. I always tried my hardest in those practice matches against him and he gave me a daily lesson. I assume I improved the following year, and he was a year older, but he still played some bloody good games. Even ten years later I believe he beat Kevin Shawcross in the best of three and Shawcross had just won the World Amateur championship. From the end of 1967 onwards I was virtually away all the time but, on the occasions that we did play in 1968, the greatest problem was always to beat him – I could never reduce him. Almost all our sessions were only 30 minutes long and increasingly we would only finish at the most two games – sensibly indecisive! He was very remarkable and I always will have the most intense respect for him and his brother Hashim. It is a shame that more of the British players haven't played Azam Khan because they would have learned an enormous amount.'

Azam Khan had better stay in training because another Barrington will soon be gunning for him. Nicholas Barrington, as we saw earlier, received his first squash racket as an eighth birthday present and is being coached by Nasrullah's son Aman, who also happens to be Azam's nephew. Who knows what the young Barrington will produce? What is certain is that he has the right blood flowing through his young veins, the genes of two successful athletes in his body, and a younger brother, Jonah Junior, who will soon be as aching to beat him as Jonah was his brother Nick all those years ago in Morwenstow. Is it not within the realms of possibility that in years to come people might be talking in as reverent tones about the Barrington dynasty as they do now about the Khans?

Jonah Barrington's Playing Career

Main Career Results compiled by **Ian Wright**,
Custodian of Records, Squash Rackets Association

Major Tournament Victories

British Open 1966–7; 1967–8; 1969–70; 1970–1; 1971–2;
1972–3
British Amateur 1966–7; 1967–8; 1968–9
Australian Amateur 1968
Australian Open 1970
Australian Professional 1970
South African Amateur 1968
Egyptian Open 1968
Pakistan Open 1970
Irish Open 1980
British Closed 1980–81

Season-by-Season

1964–5 SEASON

British Amateur   1st round: J.B. beat J.L. Moore (Australia) 9–5, 9–4, 0–9, 9–6. 2nd round: S Afifi (U.A.R.)
beat J.B. 9–7, 9–7, 9–2.

Bude Invitation Tournament Quarter-finals: J.B. beat
B.Rowlands 9–6, 9–5, 8–9, 9–6. Semi-finals: J.B. beat R.A.
Lane 9–2, 9–2, 9–2. FINAL: J.B. beat N. Barrington 9–1, 9–7,
9–1.

East of England Championships 1st round: J.B. beat D.M. Reeve 3–0. 2nd round: J.B. beat J. Woods 4–9, 9–6, 9–5, 9–3. 3rd round: J.B. beat K. Davidson 7–9, 10–8, 10–8, 9–6. 4th round: J.D. Ward beat J.B. 9–4, 9–6, 3–9, 9–2.

West of England Championships FINAL: Sharif Khan (Pakistan) beat J.B. 3–2.

Isle of Wight Championships Quarter-finals: T.D. Gathercole beat J.B. 1–9, 10–8, 1–9, 9–7, 9–3.

1965–6 SEASON

British Open 1st round: J.B. beat D.B. Hughes 9–5, 9–2, 9–7. 2nd round: T. Shafik (U.A.R.) beat J.B. 9–6, 9–6, 9–6.

British Amateur 1st round: R.M.H. Boddington beat J.B. 9–1, 9–7, 9–2.

South of England Championships 1st round: J.B. beat B.L. Ellis 9–8, 9–7, 9–2. 2nd round: J.B. beat D. White 9–6, 9–7, 9–8. 3rd round: J.B. beat D. Lock 9–1, 9–6, 9–2. Semi-finals: J.B. beat Sharif Khan (Pakistan) 9–1, 9–6, 0–9, 9–7. FINAL: J.B. beat J.D. Ward 9–7, 9–0, 10–8.

Midland Championships 1st round: J.B. beat J.B. Smith 9–3, 4–9, 3–9, 9–2, 9–6. 2nd round: J.B. beat R. Harris 9–5, 4–9, 9–3, 9–8. 3rd round: A.M.H. Hill beat J.B. 9–3, 9–6, 7–9, 9–6.

England v Ireland R.A.C. Club, London. England won 5–0. J.G.A. Lyon (1st string) beat J.B. 9–3, 8–10, 4–9, 9–5, 9–3.

Ireland v Scotland Dublin. Scotland won 4–1. O.L. Balfour (1st string) beat J.B. 9–7, 9–3, 10–9.

Ireland v Wales Dublin. Ireland won 4–1. J.B. (1st string) beat P. Stokes 9–2, 10–8, 7–9, 9–6.

North of England Championships 2nd round: J.B. beat M.R. Grundy 9–7, 9–3, 9–4. Quarter-finals: J.B. beat K.S. Davidson 9–3, 9–5, 9–1. Semi-finals: J.B. beat A. Ispahani 9–1, 9–2, 9–6. FINAL: J.B. beat Sharif Khan 7–9, 9–5, 9–4, 10–9.

West of England Championships 2nd round: J.B. beat Gulmast Khan 9–1, 9–0, 8–9, 9–5. 3rd round: J.B. beat A.M.H. Hill 9–3, 9–3, 9–3. Semi-final: J.B. beat T.C. Francis 9–5, 9–3, 9–2. FINAL: J.B. beat Sharif Khan 9–6, 9–7, 9–7.

Isle of Wight Championships Quarter-finals: J.B. beat J.F. Skinner 9–4, 9–5, 9–4. Semi-finals: J.B. beat J.D. Ward 5–9, 9–3, 9–2, 9–1. FINAL: J.B. beat T.D. Gathercole 9–1, 9–7, 9–5.

1966–7 SEASON

British Open Lansdowne & RAC Clubs 1st round: J.B. beat M.W. Corby 9–5, 7–9, 9–7, 9–4. 2nd round: J.B. beat A. Taleb* 9–4, 9–1, 8–10, 9–5. Semi-finals: J.B. beat I. Amin 9–4, 4–9, 9–5, 9–3. FINAL: J.B. beat A. Jawaid 9–2, 6–9, 9–2, 9–2.

British Amateur 1st round: J.B. beat R. Dolman 9–4, 9–5, 9–4. 2nd round: J.B. beat P. Millman 9–5, 9–2, 9–5. 3rd round: J.B. beat H. Macintosh 9–7, 9–6, 9–0.
Quarter-finals: J.B. beat J.D. Ward 9–5, 9–3, 2–0 retired.
Semi-finals: J.B. beat K. Hiscoe 5–9, 2–9, 9–5, 9–5, 9–1.
FINAL: J.B. beat R. Carter 1–9, 9–6, 7–9, 9–7, 9–0.

1967 Australia

International Championship Team Event Sydney (August)
Great Britain beat South Africa 2–1. J.B. (1st string) beat D. Botha 9–3, 9–2, 9–3.
Great Britain lost to Australia 0–3. J.B. (1st string) lost to K. Hiscoe 9–6, 9–1, 3–9, 1–9, 6–9.
Great Britain beat Pakistan 3–0. J.B. (1st string) beat M. Saleem 9–1, 9–1, 9–3.
Great Britain lost to New Zealand 1–2. J.B. (1st string) beat C. Waugh 9–4, 9–0, 9–4.

International Championship Individual Event 1st round: J. B. beat G. Clements (Victoria) 9–1, 9–5, 9–3. 2nd round:

---

* Although invariably referred to as Abou Taleb, his correct name was A. Abou Taleb (he died in 1983).

J.B. beat M. Simons (Victoria) 9–3, 9–6, 9–5. 3rd round: J.B. beat E. Hamilton (N.S.W.) 9–0, 9–2, 9–2. Quarter-finals: J.B. beat D. Botha (S.A.) 9–7, 10–9, 9–1. Semi-finals: C. Nancarrow (N.S.W.) beat J. B. 9–7, 9–6, 9–7.

1967–8 SEASON

British Open Lansdowne & RAC Clubs (December) 1st round: J.B. beat A.M.H. Hill 9–7, 9–3, 9–5. 2nd round: J. B. beat D. Brazier 9–2, 9–7, 9–5. Semi-finals: J.B. beat K. Zaghloul 9–2, 9–2, 9–0. FINAL: J.B. beat A. Taleb 9–6, 9–0, 9–5.

British Amateur RAC & Lansdowne Clubs (January) 1st round: J. B. beat J.S.W. Hunt 9–3, 9–5, 9–0. 2nd round: J.B. beat R.A.G. White 9–2, 9–2, 9–2. 3rd round: J.B. beat B. Leibenburg 9–5, 9–0, 9–3. Quarter-finals: J.B. beat D.B. Hughes 9–6, 9–5, 9–1. Semi-finals: J.B. beat A.M.H. Hill 9–1, 9–2, 9–0. FINAL: J.B. beat M.W. Corby 9–3, 9–6, 2–9, 9–5.

1968 Egypt

Egyptian Open Cairo (March) FINAL: J.B. beat A. Taleb 9–4, 9–2, 9–7.

1968 South Africa

South African Championships (July) 3rd round: J.B. beat N. Liberman 9–1, 9–1, 9–3. 4th round: J.B. beat D. Quail 9–3, 9–6, 9–2. Semi-finals: J.B. beat Doug Barrow 9–0, 9–3, 9–2. FINAL: J.B. beat Dave Barrow 9–3, 9–2, 9–0.

1968 Australia

Australian Amateur Championships Perth (August) 3rd round: J. B. beat F. Taafe 9–4, 9–0, 9–5. 4th round: J.B. beat R. Carter 9–1, 9–5, 9–2. Semi-finals: J.B. beat G. Hunt 9–4, 9–2, 4–9, 6–9, 9–6. FINAL: J.B. beat K. Hiscoe 4–9, 9–2, 9–5, 4–9, 9–2.

1968–9 SEASON

British Amateur RAC & Lansdowne Clubs (December) 1st round: J. B. beat N.J. Barrington 7–9, 9–4, 9–4, 9–6. 2nd round: J.B. beat P.E. Goodwin 9–7, 9–4, 9–3. 3rd round: J.B. beat S.A. Ispahani 9–2, 9–1, 9–6. Quarter-finals: J.B. beat J.D. Ward 7–9, 10–8, 9–7, 9–1. Semi-finals: J.B. beat P. Millman 9–4, 9–0, 9–0. FINAL: J.B. beat M.W. Corby 3–9, 9–1, 9–2, 9–3.

British Open Abbeydale Park, Sheffield (January) 1st round: J.B. beat K.S. Davidson 9–1, 9–0, 9–2. 2nd round: J.B. beat R.N. Lewis 9–1, 9–2, 9–3. Quarter-finals: J.B. beat A.M.H. Hill 9–3, 9–4, 9–2. Semi-finals: C. Nancarrow beat J.B. 9–4, 9–5, 10–8.

World Amateur Championship Team Event (February)
Great Britain lost to Australia 1–2. J.B. (1st string) beat G. Hunt 2–9, 9–4, 8–10, 9–4, 9–7.
Great Britain beat South Africa 3–0. J.B. (1st string) beat D. Botha 9–4, 9–0, 9–3.
Great Britain beat Pakistan 2–1. J.B. (1st string) beat A. Jawaid 2–9, 9–5, 4–9, 9–3, 10–8.
Great Britain beat U.A.R. 2–1. J.B. (1st string) beat S. Afifi 9–5, 9–1, 9–6.
Great Britain beat New Zealand 2–1. J.B. (1st string) beat T. Johnston 9–4, 9–0, 9–3.

World Amateur Championships Individual Event (February) 1st round: J.B. beat D. Botha 9–0, 9–5, 9–4. 2nd round: J.B. beat P. Dibley 9–2, 9–1, 9–2. 3rd round: J.B. beat P. Kirton 9–1, 9–0, 9–3. Quarter-finals: J.B. beat T. Johnston 9–7, 9–1, 9–2. Semi-finals: J.B. beat C. Nancarrow 9–0, 9–2, 10–8. FINAL: G. Hunt beat J.B. 9–7, 2–9, 9–4, 9–0.

1969–70 SEASON

British Open Edgbaston Priory, Birmingham (December) 1st round: J.B. beat D.M. Innes 7–9, 9–4, 9–7, 9–1. 2nd round: J.B. beat J.N.C. Easter 9–6, 9–1, 9–4. Semi-finals: J.B. beat M. Yasin 9–5, 6–9, 9–5, 9–3. FINAL: J.B. beat G. Hunt 9–7, 3–9, 3–9, 9–4, 9–4.

1970 Pakistan

Pakistan Open (Feb-March) FINAL: J. B. beat A. Jawaid

1970 Australia

Australian Professional Championships Semi-finals: J.B. beat K. Parker (N.S.W.) 9–2, 9–3, 9–3. FINAL: J.B. beat T. Hosford (N.S.W.) 9–1, 9–6, 9–5.

Australian Open Albert Park, Melbourne 1st round: J.B. beat R. Lewis (Vict.) 9–3, 7–9, 4–9, 9–7, 9–5. Quarter-finals: J.B. beat D. Stephenson (S. Aust.) 9–0, 8–10, 9–6, 9–4. Semi-finals: J.B. beat L. Robberds (N.S.W.) 9–4, 9–2, 2–9, 9–3. FINAL: J.B. beat G. Hunt (Vict.) 9–2, 6–9, 6–9, 9–3, 9–3.

1970–1 SEASON

British Open Edgbaston Priory (December) 2nd round: J.B. beat G. Alauddin 9–4, 9–0, 9–0. 3rd round: J.B. beat T.C. Francis 9–0, 9–0, 9–2. Quarter-finals: J.B. beat M.Z. Hepker 9–2, 9–1, 9–0. Semi-finals: J.B. beat Sharif Khan 9–0, 9–7, 3–9, 9–3. FINAL: J.B. beat A. Jawaid 9–1, 9–2, 9– 6.

1971–2 SEASON

British Open Abbeydale Park (January–February) 1st round: J.B. beat A. Nadi 9–3, 9–0, 9–1. 2nd round: J.B. beat P. de Semlyen 9–2, 9–1, 9–3. 3rd round: J.B. beat R. Lewis 9–4, 9–0, 9–5. 4th round: J.B. beat G. Allam 9–6, 9– 3, 9–7. Semi-finals: J.B. beat G. Alauddin 10–8, 9–7, 9–2. FINAL: J.B. beat G. Hunt 0–9, 9–7, 10–8, 6–9, 9–7.

1972–3 SEASON

British Open Abbeydale Park (January–February) 1st round: J.B. beat B. Patterson 9–0, 9–7, 9–6. 2nd round: J.B. beat A. Khan 9–6, 5–9, 9–4, 9–3. 3rd round: J.B. beat J. Easter 9–4, 8–10, 9–2, 9–1. 4th round: J.B. beat A. Safwat 9–3, 9–4, 9–10, 9–0. Semi-finals: J.B. beat K. Hiscoe 3–9, 9–1, 7–9, 9–1, 9–2. FINAL: J.B. beat G. Alauddin 9–4, 9–3, 9–2.

1973–4 SEASON

Benson & Hedges British Open Abbeydale Park, Sheffield (February) 1st round: J.B. beat P. Kirton 9–1, 9–4, 9–6. 2nd round: J.B. beat J. Easter 9–6, 10–9, 10–9. 3rd round: J.B. beat P. Ayton 0–9, 9–3, 9–5, 10–8. 4th round: M. Yasin beat J.B. 1–9, 9–4, 10–8, 9–2.

1974 South Africa

South African Open Johannesburg (August–September) Quarter-finals: J.B. beat K.J. Hiscoe 9–5, 9–6, 9–1. Semi-finals: G. Hunt beat J.B. 9–4, 9–7, 0–9, 9–4.

1974–5 SEASON

Benson & Hedges Open Championship Wembley (January–February) 1st round: J.B. beat K. Bruce-Lockhart 9–5, 9–2, 9–1. 2nd round: J.B. beat P. Wright 9–0, 9–0, 9–1. 3rd round: J.B. beat M. Yasin 9–4, 9–3, 9–4. Quarter-finals: G. Alauddin beat J.B. 9–3, 9–6, 9–0.

Great Britain v Pakistan Open International Wembley G.B. lost 0–5. G. Alauddin beat J.B. 9–1, 9–7, 8–10, 9–6.

1975 South Africa

South Africa Open Johannesburg (August–September) Quarter-finals: C. Nancarrow beat J.B. 9–6, 10–8, 5–9, 9–6.

1975–6 SEASON

Lucas British Open Wembley Squash Centre (January–February) 1st round: J.B. beat B. Patterson 9–3, 9–3, 9–3. 2nd round: J.B. beat M. Grundy 9–1, 9–5, 9–5. 3rd round: J.B. beat M. Yasin 5–9, 10–8, 9–1, 9–4. Quarter-finals: Q. Zaman beat J.B. 9–0, 9–1, 9–6.

1976 South Africa

South African Open Quarter-finals: J.B. beat A.A. Aziz 7–9, 9–4, 9–5, 5–9, 9–7. Semi-finals: C. Nancarrow beat J.B. 9–4, 9–5, 10–9.

1976–7 SEASON

Lucas British Open Wembley Squash Centre (March–April) 1st round: J.B. beat E. Berry 9–5, 9–3, 9–7. 2nd round: J.B. beat W. Skinner 9–1, 9–1, 9–1. 3rd round: J.B. beat A. Kaoud 10–9, 9–4, 9–3. Quarter-finals: J.B. beat R. Watson 10–8, 9–1, 5–9, 9–6. Semi-finals: G. Hunt beat J.B. 9–5, 9–2, 9–0.

1977–8 SEASON

Avis British Open Wembley Squash Centre (March–April) 1st round: J.B. beat M. Helal 10–8, 9–5, 9–2. 2nd round: J.B. beat M. Khalifa 9–1, 9–2, 9–1. 3rd round: J.B. beat A. Safwat 9–7, 3–9, 10–8, 4–9, 9–0. Quarter-finals: G. Hunt beat J.B. 9–3, 9–2, 9–5.

1978–9 SEASON

Avis British Open Wembley Squash Centre (March–April) 1st round: J.B. beat N. Zahran 9–1, 9–0, 9–1. 2nd round: J.B. beat S. Bowditch 9–0, 5–9, 9–5, 9–5. 3rd round: J.B. beat R. Watson 7–9, 9–1, 9–2, 9–4. Quarter-finals: H. Jahan beat J.B. 9–0, 9–4, 9–3.

1979–80 SEASON

Avis British Open Championship 1st round: J.B. beat M. Khalifa 9–1, 9–1, 9–2. 2nd round: J.B. beat G. Dupré 9–1, 9–6, 9–5. 3rd round: J.B. beat J. Khan 9–3, 4–9, 9–7, 9–0. Quarter-finals: G. Hunt beat J.B. 9–3, 9–2, 7–9, 9–6.

Irish Open (May) FINAL: J.B. beat Jahangir Khan.

1980–1 SEASON

Thornton's British Closed Championship (December) 2nd round: J.B. beat B. Patterson 9–4, 9–0, 9–0. 3rd round: J.B. beat S. Bateman 9–6, 9–0, 9–0. Quarter-finals: J.B. beat J. Le Lievre 7–9, 9–2, 9–3, 9–0. Semi-finals: J.B. beat P. Kenyon 9–1, 5–9, 9–3, 9–6. FINAL: J.B. beat G. Briars 4–9, 9–3, 9–0, 9–2.

Index

Index

EVERYTHING YOU NEED TO KNOW ABOUT SPORT (AND A LOT OF THINGS YOU DON'T)!

The Book Of

SPORTS
LISTS

CRAIG AND DAVID BROWN

Who 'floats like a butterfly and stings like one too'?
Who gave up sex for a year in order to improve his game
– and what does it cost to persuade John McEnroe to
play with your racquets for a year? Which sportsman
said 'I'd give my right arm to be a pianist' – and what do
Torvill and Dean have to say about each other?

THE BOOK OF SPORTS LISTS brings together the
most remarkable things ever done and the funniest
things ever said in the name of sport around the world.
Record-breakers and blunderers, prudes and Casanovas,
good sports and bad sports, they're all in THE BOOK OF
SPORTS LISTS.

NON-FICTION/HUMOUR/SPORT　　0 7221 1935 6　　£2.50

*Don't miss Craig Brown and Lesley Cunliffe's THE
BOOK OF ROYAL LISTS, also available in Sphere
Books.*

As real as today's headlines – and even more shocking . . .

MONIMBÓ

ROBERT MOSS AND ARNAUD DE BORCHGRAVE

Bestselling authors of The Spike

July 1980: at a secret meeting in Monimbo, Nicaragua, Fidel
Castro unveils a devastating Kremlin-backed masterplan to
unleash bloodshed and chaos on the streets of America.

Among Washington's Press corps, only Robert Hockney dares
to suspect Cuban intentions. But will he survive long enough
to break the story? And can one man's warning voice halt
America's countdown to doomsday?

From the violent underworld of Miami terrorism to the deadly
realities of political terrorism, MONIMBO is a searing attack
on Western complacency and a blockbusting novel of
suspense, action and intrigue.

'Fast-paced and thought-provoking.' *Henry Kissinger.*

ADVENTURE THRILLER   0 7221 1865 1   £2.25

The explosive new thriller of World War II's most
baffling enigma

THE JUDAS CODE
DEREK LAMBERT

Bestselling author of I, SAID THE SPY

A journalist advertises for information about the key to
the Judas Code. An elderly gentleman turns up at his
flat and threatens to kill him. But the journalist
nevertheless manages to meet someone who tells him
the story . . .

Hitler, Churchill and Stalin are all involved in a tale of
intrigue and double-cross on an unrivalled scale. A
young Czech in neutral Lisbon, a British intelligence
agent operative of very divided loyalties and a beautiful
Jewess are all manipulated by a master planner, in a
breathtaking scheme to propel Russia and Germany into
conflict, buying the Allies the most precious commodity
of all: time.

'Mr. Lambert is .... very informed about the known facts
of the war into which he weaves his fantasy.' *Daily
Telegraph*.

'Lambert certainly keeps the action moving.' *Liverpool
Daily Post*.

FICTION/ADVENTURE THRILLER   0 7221 5350 3   £2.25

*Pick up the pulse-pounding action where
FIREFOX left off . . .*

FIREFOX DOWN

Craig Thomas

Bestselling author of FIREFOX

FIREFOX IS MISSING . . .
EVERYONE WANTS IT BACK . . .
THE RACE IS *ON* TO RECOVER THE FIREFOX!

FIREFOX: the NATO codename for a supersonic Soviet warplane so
deadly it can wipe the West out of the skies.

Stolen for the West by ace U.S. pilot Mitchell Gant, the Firefox is shot
down in a hair-raising dogfight. Now the plane lies submerged
beneath the icy waters of a frozen Finnish lake, waiting to be salvaged
by British Intelligence. And Mitchell Gant is running for his life, from
the tracker dogs and helicopter patrols of the KGB border guard. As
international tension mounts, East and West wage a desperate
offstage battle – a frantic race to FIND THE FIREFOX!

ADVENTURE/THRILLER   0 7221 8449 2   £2.25

Also by Craig Thomas and in Sphere paperback:

FIREFOX   SEA LEOPARD   RAT TRAP
SNOW FALCON   WOLFSBANE   JADE TIGER

A SELECTION OF BESTSELLERS FROM SPHERE

FICTION

SMART WOMEN	Judy Blume	£2.25 □
INHERITORS OF THE STORM	Victor Sondheim	£2.95 □
HEADLINES	Bernard Weinraub	£2.75 □
TRINITY'S CHILD	William Prochnau	£2.50 □
THE SINISTER TWILIGHT	J. S. Forrester	£1.95 □

FILM & TV TIE-INS

WATER	Gordon McGill	£1.75 □
THE RADISH DAY JUBILEE	Sheilah B. Bruce	£1.50 □
THE RIVER	Steven Bauer	£1.95 □
THE DUNE STORYBOOK	Joan D. Vinge	£2.50 □
ONCE UPON A TIME IN AMERICA	Lee Hays	£1.75 □

NON-FICTION

THE *WOMAN* BOOK OF LOVE AND SEX	Deidre Sanders	£1.95 □
PRINCESS GRACE	Steven Englund	£2.50 □
MARGARET RUTHERFORD – A BLITHE SPIRIT	Dawn Langley Simmons	£1.95 □
BARRY FANTONI'S CHINESE HOROSCOPES	Barry Fantoni	£1.75 □
THE STEP-PARENT'S HANDBOOK	Elizabeth Hodder	£2.95 □

All Sphere books are available at your local bookshop or newsagent, or can be ordered direct from the publisher. Just tick the titles you want and fill in the form below.

Name_____

Address_____

_____

Write to Sphere Books, Cash Sales Department, P.O. Box 11, Falmouth, Cornwall TR10 9EN

Please enclose cheque or postal order to the value of the cover price plus:

UK: 55p for the first book, 22p for the second book and 14p per copy for each additional book ordered to a maximum charge of £1.75.

OVERSEAS: £1.00 for the first book and 25p per copy for each additional book.

BFPO & EIRE: 55p for the first book, 22p for the second book plus 14p per copy for the next 7 books, thereafter 8p per book.

Sphere Books reserve the right to show new retail prices on covers which may differ from those previously advertised in the text or elsewhere, and to increase postal rates in accordance with the PO.